Mr. Galloway Goes to Washington

Mr. Galloway Goes to Washington

to Washington

The Brit Who Set Congress Straight About Iraq

George Galloway

THE NEW PRESS

NEW YORK
LONDON

Requests for permission to reproduce selections from this book should
be mailed to: Permissions Department, The New Press, 38 Greene
Street, New York, NY 10013

Published in the United States by The New Press, New York, 2005
Distributed by W. W. Norton & Company, Inc., New York

ISBN 1-59558-062-X
CIP data available

The New Press was established in 1990 as a not-for-profit alternative to
the large, commercial publishing houses currently dominating the book
publishing industry. The New Press operates in the public interest rather
than for private gain, and is committed to publishing, in innovative
ways, works of educational, cultural, and community value that are often
deemed insufficiently profitable.

www.thenewpress.com

Composition by dix!

Printed in the United States of America

10   9   8   7   6   5   4   3   2   1

CONTENTS

Mr. Galloway Goes
to Washington

SADDAM AND ME

Frankly it was the last call in the world I wanted to take. It was a famous and glamorous Arab film star who called me up out of the blue as I sat in the Lebanese capital Beirut in the Spring of 2004. Although I would have been pleased to see her, it was definitely not a "come up and see me sometime" sort of call.

She was telephoning, she said, for a cousin of Saddam Hussein. Saddam needed my help—to find a lawyer to save him from the hangman's noose. My heart sank.

I knew that her calls were almost certainly monitored—she is a well-known dissident in her country. I figured any cousin of prisoner No. 1 in Cell-Block Iraq was likely to be monitored also. And I have always proceeded on the basis that "Big Brother" is watching me.

I wanted to say "Why me?" but she was already into an explanation. He wants an English Queens Counsel, she said. He respects the British legal system and he thought I would know the right person to approach. I could have said no but I did not, for several reasons.

Saddam Hussein could have had no legitimate complaint if, having lived by the sword—ruthlessly cutting down any and all opposition—he had died by the sword at the hands of Iraqis. But that was not the situation. No trial arranged by an occupying army could have any validity in law. Nothing legal could come from the invasion of Iraq carried out in flagrant defiance of the United Nations. The people who deserved to be on trial for crimes against the Iraqi people were first and foremost George Bush and Tony Blair. Saddam had committed many awful acts against his people, most of them at a time when I was demonstrating against him and when he was a highly profitable client of the same Anglo-American axis now holding him, but their crimes were greater than his.

The so-called "governing council"—that fiction of a government in Baghdad—was not entitled to take any action in the country. This was not the government of Iraq; it had been imposed by the tanks, guns and planes of foreign invaders. Most of its members were little more than "foreigners." Some had left Iraq as much as forty years before and could walk down any street in Baghdad without being recognized. And some were criminals themselves, like the chief American stooge Ahmad Chalabi. In 1992 the U.S. government paid for the creation of the Iraqi National Congress (INC)—even inventing its name. It was given $12 million over the next four years to organize itself under Chalabi's leadership.

Scion of a hugely wealthy Shiite landowning family, Chalabi, acting in league with the British-created monarchy, had established the Petra Bank—the second biggest in Jordan—in 1977. In 1989 King Hussein's Jordanian government was forced to seize the bank and inject $164 million to avert its collapse and a resulting financial meltdown of Jordan's whole banking system. Chalabi—for a time paraded as a future U.S.-imposed "president" of Iraq, one of the world's most oil rich countries—escaped the kingdom in the trunk of a car. He was subsequently tried in absentia and sentenced to 22 years' hard labor in prison for embezzlement, fraud and currency trading irregularities. Though the Jordanian government claimed he escaped with over $70 million, there has recently been discussion of an official pardon. Chalabi was distrusted by the State Department and the CIA. But in the eyes of the Pentagon and the neo-cons like Rumsfeld, Wolfowitz and Perle who control it, he repaid the U.S. investment in him by persuading the fools on the Hill in Washington that the Iraqi people would welcome an invasion.

That George Bush, the man who had done so much to wreck the international criminal court, should not only try and convict someone in a country he'd invaded but also, in a TV interview the night before my telephone call from the actress, actually pass sentence (death; his favorite verdict executed well over a hundred times during his governorship of Texas)—the very idea made me sick to the stomach.

All accused persons have the right to the best defense possible, in the view of just people at least. It is one of the things that should distinguish us from prison-states like Saddam's Iraq. Touched by the dictator's apparent belief that Britain had the best lawyers, I made a call to the well-known British barrister Michael Mansfield.

He was in Belfast—he has been a major player in the Bloody Sunday inquiry into the events more than thirty years ago in Derry—and didn't get back to me until the next day. He suspected—as I knew he would—that I would pass on to him an offer to take up the highest-profile legal case in the whole world. Not that he was short of them at that moment—that very day the long-awaited inquest into the death of Princess Diana and Dodi al Fayed had been announced. Mansfield was, he said, acting for Mohamed al Fayed, Dodi's father and Arab "conspiracy theorist" par excellence (he believes the Duke of Edinburgh had Diana murdered because she was carrying a Muslim child).

Mansfield is a man of the left with a long record of defending unpopular clients. In the best traditions of the English bar, he gives his (considerable) all for whomsoever he's representing. He was clearly interested in some level of involvement in the case, despite his enormous workload. But he mentioned that the other "silks" (Queens Counsels) in his chambers were outstanding figures whom he was sure would be interested in more front-line involvement in the case. I inferred from this that he would have a semi-detached role to play, which cooled my interest a little. I had envisaged him, sword of justice in hand, as the best possible representative. He mentioned—because he thought the potential client might want to know—that the colleagues he had in mind were Jewish. I told him I was sure this would constitute no barrier. Whatever his other sins, Saddam Hussein is a secular man who ruthlessly suppressed Islamic fundamentalists in his country. His Ba'ath party is a mixture of Arab nationalism and Stalinist authoritarianism. He hates Israel, no doubt, but in my experience none of the Ba'ath leaders had ever displayed any hostility to Jews.

That phone call from the film actress had made my heart sink for another reason. It confirmed something I would rather have forgotten. Saddam Hussein and George Galloway were, it seemed, doomed to be an item. Saddam and me—we go way back.

There has been no other Arab ruler whom I have more mercilessly attacked, about whom I've made more scathing comments, against whom I have campaigned more energetically.

When hardly anyone knew Saddam's name, I was disseminating literature, drawing (or rather failing in my attempt to draw) attention to his crimes. I had met him only twice, and one of those occasions was as part of a large group. In parliament—therefore in the public record—on television, in the press, and at public meetings I have carpet-bombed the record of Saddam Hussein, both before and since I met him for the first time in 1994. But what I said on the occasion of that early visit to Baghdad has made it much easier ever since for my enemies to grotesquely caricature my views.

"Sir, I salute your courage, your strength, your indefatigability."

How many times have I had those words rammed down my throat by people with not a scintilla of my record on human rights and democracy in Iraq? How much do I regret the potential for damage in that brief statement? How long have you got?

Just a couple of months before the visit on which I delivered this greeting, I had described in parliament the regime in Baghdad as a "bestial dictatorship." And here I was, apparently praising the very same regime, in the beast's own Tikriti lair.

The "your" in question in those remarks is not a singular possessive but a plural. Those being praised for their courage strength and indefatigability (one of the strange archaic English words my brain persists in throwing up and which I am sure no Iraqi translator had ever interpreted before) are the 23 million Iraqis, not their president. As a correspondent to the letters columns of the *Guardian* newspaper pointed out at the time, the comment burst like a bombshell in the British media; if I'd used the good old Scottish word "youse" instead of "your" the ruthlessly exploited misinterpretation of my comments would have been disabled. But in any event I should have known better. I badly misjudged the way in which those comments could be taken out of context. I have given literally thousands of speeches and interviews in my time and not always of the same quality.

I am an emotional person and the couple of weeks before the interview had been a roller-coaster. I had come to Iraq from Palestine, always an emotionally charged tour in the prison camp that is the Occupied Territories. The bitter and brutal reality of the life of the captive Palestinian people there was weighing heavily on me. And Iraq itself, especially in 1994, fully two years before the first Oil-for-Food program, was simply a sea of misery. It is hard now to convey the shock and awe inspired by a tour of the Iraqi killing fields when the country was under total siege. The mass grave of those slaughtered by sanctions is yet to be uncovered by most of the Western media and politicians. But it will be when journalism—history's first draft—gives way to the real thing. An Iraqi child was dying at the rate of one every six seconds then—a rate of attrition which dwarfs any of the crimes of Saddam. Most of these children died before they even knew that they were Iraqis. Yet they died for no other reason than that they *were* Iraqis—and small and vulnerable ones, about whom few outside the Muslim world cared a fig. The day before the ill-fated meeting in Tikrit—to which we had been conducted in circumstances of great secrecy—I had listened at the door of a labor ward while a woman gave birth by Caesarean section, without anesthetic. At the meeting with Saddam I allowed my emotions to run away with me. I said things in a way I shouldn't have. Only a fool has no regrets. And I will regret the gift I inadvertently gave my enemies, always.

I set off the night of the meeting, across the long desert road from Baghdad to Jordan and a flight home, completely oblivious to any damage that I had caused. I arrived in the early morning at the airport in Amman, weary and bedraggled. At Heathrow airport in London I was met at the door of the plane by an official of the airline who passed me a note from a BBC journalist friend in Scotland, warning me that the media had gone bananas and was waiting for me. I still did not know what for. As I was reading the note I was aware of a flash, then another, then another. Paparazzi had, presumably improperly, gotten airside and were now swarming all around me. I kept my head up and walked as tall as I could, my mind spinning, trying to work out what had happened. It was not until I walked out into the arrivals hall amid a huge scrum of cameras journalists and film crews and was asked the first questions that I knew what all the fuss was about.

At the same time my flat in Glasgow, where my wife was studying for her PhD, was under siege. Journalists were making the usual, paid, offers for her to "tell her side of the story," promising a sympathetic hearing of course. Showing the casual racism commonplace in the media, because she was an Arab they inferred she must be an Iraqi. In fact, they asked her if it was true she was the niece of Saddam Hussein!

Hilariously, that day my office had asked for the

shop where we rented our television to send an engineer to fix an erratic picture. When the man arrived my wife shouted through the door, "Who is it?"

"It's the TV man," he replied.

"I have no comment to make," she retorted, perhaps the strangest ever response from a customer wanting their TV fixed.

The whole affair felt like picking up a live electricity cable and I was burned very badly. Foolishly I asked some Iraqi kids in Britain to write to my daughter Lucy, knowing she was taking some stick at school, to encourage her and set out the defense of what I had done. She was furious with me, implying as it did the possibility of disloyalty on her part. She was twelve years old. My friends in my constituency remained absolutely solid and the electorate in Glasgow would later double my parliamentary majority (a fact strangely missed by the legion of commentators who had predicted my certain defeat in the wake of the row). The atmosphere elsewhere can be judged however by the fact that my account of the meeting, written under total media siege and for which I was paid thousands of pounds by a newspaper, was never published.

In the aftermath of the row I felt my usefulness on the Iraq issue had come to an end. Continued campaigning on the subject would, I felt, not only be bad for me but useless for the Iraqis. I was damaged goods, at least as far as the issue was concerned, and perhaps in general too. I quietly informed the then Iraqi Chargé d'Affaires Zuhair Ibrahim and my Iraqi friends in Britain that I was retiring, hurt, from this particular battlefield.

People often asked me, then and later, what Saddam had been like. In a way, how could I know? I had less than two minutes of face time with him and had merely participated in a staged "dialogue" with dozens of others. In any case I came to realize that people did not really want to hear what, in that limited exposure, he had actually been "like." They merely wanted their prejudices confirmed.

But for what it is now worth, he was not what I expected. He was not loud, bombastic, aggressive or intimidating. His handshake was soft, not the vise-like grip I expected. I formed the impression—buttressed on my second meeting with him eight years later—that he was actually rather shy, avoiding people's gaze, looking down at his chest, speaking softly. He appeared touched by the enormous volume of good wishes I had been asked to convey to him from the young people of the Intifada raging in Palestine. Virtually alone of all the Arab dictators, Saddam's endless protestations of fidelity to the Palestinian cause were sincere and, as the families of the martyred and wounded in the Intifada know, he put Iraq's money where his mouth was.

He spoke in a monotonous yet oddly charismatic way. Perhaps something was lost in the translation, but what he said struck me as messianic rubbish. His droning on about good caliphs and bad ones made little sense to a group of Europeans, without any real grasp of the ancient Arab and Islamic history he was drawing on. The surprise of this was compounded when he interrupted the meeting to go off and pray.

Iraq, formerly a bastion of secular "socialism," had made a belated turn to God. A Koranic invocation "Allah o Akhbar" (God is Great) had been inscribed on their flag, and Saddam had begun making a point of going off ostentatiously to pray. Alcohol had been banned in public places (though the important Christian population was allowed to continue to buy and sell it to other non-Muslims) which must have been a wrench to Saddam himself;

he famously liked a glass of Mateus Rose wine with his dinner. All of this was a politically inspired turn to win the hearts of the broader Muslim world and to further marginalize the Saudi regime next door, who sought to portray themselves as worthy custodians of the two mosques at Mecca and Medina.

I next set foot in Iraq in 1998. Having been triumphantly re-elected (despite the ruthlessly used Saddam quotes deployed by my electoral opponents) the year before, and painfully conscious of the constant though still scarcely known suffering of the Iraqi people, I felt it was time to return to the battle.

The first person I met on my return was the then-foreign minister Tariq Aziz. I had flown in a helicopter with him to the Tikrit meeting with Saddam four years earlier. But it was on that trip in 1998 that I formed a lasting bond with him. Though it might profit me to do so, I am not the sort of person to turn my back on my friends, especially when they are in the sort of trouble he is now in. I grew to admire and like Tariq Aziz, as many, like Douglas Hurd, the Pope, even Donald Rumsfeld, had done before me. He is a truly impressive man, with a good, devoutly Catholic family. He had started life as a journalist and ended as the deputy prime minister of

Iraq. There was no prime minister. Only Saddam was *primus inter pares*. Aziz was for many years Iraq's voice in the outside world. His owlish intellectualism and his impeccable manners made him the ideal counterpoint to the unworldly, little-traveled and uncouth Saddam.

My wife's uncle, the writer Said Abu-Rish, is the biographer of Saddam Hussein. In his book Abu-Rish identifies the many ways in which Saddam resembles Joseph Stalin (apart from the moustache). Both came from, literally, dirt-poor backgrounds. I mean houses with earth floors. Neither knew their fathers. Both had mothers who drove them ever onwards and upwards by sheer will and sacrifice. Both were determined to industrialize their countries, at whatever the cost. Both had a chip on their shoulder. Both built police states believing the end justified the means. Both ruthlessly suppressed all tendencies towards the breakup of their country, believing in a strong central authority (themselves). Both were outsiders in their system— Stalin the Russified Georgian who never quite lost his rough edges, Saddam the barefoot boy from the backward backwater of Tikrit selling cigarettes from a tray. Both rose to the top ahead of more gifted, more sophisticated, better loved figures in their party. And both, of course, could be murderous in pursuit of their goals. An important difference however was that Stalin was as cautious in his foreign policy as Saddam was reckless.

This brings us to another set of uncomfortable truths. Neither Stalin nor Saddam Hussein were psychopaths, driven by some inner compulsion to be cruel for no reason. Saddam's crimes, like Stalin's, were first committed against his own comrades. His purges of the party began after several years as deputy president when he finally moved aside the president and took the top job he was already in practice occupying. He knew that there was a faction at the top of the Iraqi section of the Ba'ath party, close to neighboring Syria, which stood as a barrier to his absolute control of the party. In authoritarian societies such a stand-off only ends one way, with the deaths of one or other faction. Stalin gave his factional opponents a show trial and then killed them. Saddam just killed them.

Only months after Saddam's absorption of total power he decided upon the first of his reckless un-Stalin-like adventures—the attempt to overthrow Khomeini and defeat the Islamic revolution in Iran. In this gamble he had the wholehearted backing of Britain, America, and the Gulf Arab satrapies that trembled before Khomeini's rage.

I opposed this war, and when it started, followed Syria in supporting Iran. I abhorred the carnage created by the First World War-style attrition that the war involved. Not so the very Axis powers who now wish to add it to Saddam's charge sheet. For example, take the infamous Halabja incident where, it must be presumed, Iraqi forces fired chemical weapons into a Kurdish village, killing a large number of civilians including many children. Saddam had chemical weapons because the West—the U.S. and its then close ally West Germany in particular—supplied them to him. U.S. Defense secretary Donald Rumsfeld went to Baghdad, twice, to help Saddam use his weapons more effectively. For many months after Halabja the U.S. State Department, in publicly available documents, insisted that this crime was committed by Khomeini, not Saddam. Long after Halabja both Britain and America continued to arm and support Saddam against Iran. Now, having changed the identity of the perpetrator and inflated the number of victims from 400 to 8,000, they wish to hang Saddam for a war-crime in which they were deeply complicit. This was implicitly recognized by the treatment of the affair in the stooge media where hands were regularly thrown up in horror about Halabja.

The American authors Sheldon Rampton and John Stauber, in their wonderful short book *Weapons of Mass Deception: The Uses of Propaganda in Bush's War on Iraq,* did an internet search of the mentions of Halabja in the Western media. It makes grimly comic reading. In 1988, the year of the incident, when the memory of U.S. support for Saddam was as fresh as the graves of those gassed Kurds, the incident was mentioned 188 times in U.S. articles. It was cited 20 times in 1989 and 29 times in 1990, the year of the Kuwait invasion. During the whole of the period between August 2, 1990 and the end of the first Iraq war on February 27, 1991, Halabja was mentioned only 39 times. During the subsequent decade it averaged only 16 mentions a year in all U.S. media. During the U.S. presidential election year 2000 it got only ten mentions. After George Bush decided upon his attack on Iraq, however, mentions of Halabja increased sharply. In February 2003 alone it was mentioned 57 times. In March 145 times. Fifteen years after the attack and with faded memories of whose side the U.S. had been on at the time, it was suddenly in vogue to care about the Kurds at Halabja. Virtually none of the reports, however, even mentioned that at the time of the massacre of Halabja's children, George Bush's father was U.S. vice-president in an administration that had been showering their killers with financial aid.

Saddam's gassing of the Kurds in 1988 was pre-figured more than sixty years before when another government sought to crush a rebellion in Iraq by rebel northern tribesmen. The tribesmen were Kurds, the government that dropped chemical gas on them was British. Speaking in parliament the minister responsible, one Winston Churchill, said, "I can't understand this squeamishness about the use of gas against uncivilized tribes."

Churchill, it emerged after the Second World War, had laid in a huge arsenal of chemical and bio-logical weapons along the channel coast which, of course, he would have unleashed if Hitler's army had landed. I still await an answer to a question which has bothered me for years: why are some people al-lowed to have, even use, weapons of mass destruc-tion while others are not?

Iraqi society remained remarkably solid during

the eight long years of war with Iran. The Shiite majority in Iraq proved that they were Arabs and Iraqis first and co-religionists of Khomeini second. But there was a fifth column, Shiite elements who actively undermined the Iraqi war effort in the interests of their country's enemy. As in all authoritarian societies this fifth column was ruthlessly annihilated wherever it was found. Some of the graves of these victims are now being uncovered with hypocritical glee by the very governments which helped Saddam's insane invasion of Iran in the first place.

Why, I asked the leaders of Iraq, did you weaken both of your countries, lose the lives of a million souls, and beggar both economies? Why didn't you unite with Iran and challenge the slave dictatorships in the Gulf? You could have changed the world. That is my world view; it is not, of course, that of Bush and Blair.

The Iraqi answer was always the same: Khomeini was not interested in an alliance with an Arab nationalist secularist government. They would have exported their Islamic fundamentalist revolution to us. We acted against them before they got a chance to act against us. And we "won" the war. Khomeini was stopped in his tracks. This is, of course, just what the West intended.

The next big crime of which Saddam Hussein stands accused is the putting down of the uprisings in both the north and south of the country in the immediate aftermath of the 1991 war. These uprisings, a revolutionary struggle for power and for the overthrow of the government, involved massive violence on both sides—as any civil war does. Large numbers of local Ba'athist officials and their families were massacred in the south by the Shiite uprising. Many were thrown from tall buildings to their death and then their corpses danced upon. But Saddam's regime had the greater firepower and, once the uprising had been betrayed by Bush Senior, who had called on the people to rise up then abandoned them, the result was inevitable. Saddam crushed his enemies without mercy.

In the north, the Kurdish forces sought to use the enfeeblement of the Baghdad regime to finally be free and to set up the state of Kurdistan they have coveted for so long. The West has never supported the creation of such a Kurdish state though they have sometimes pretended to do so. Such a state would instantly destabilize their NATO ally Turkey, which has brutally suppressed Kurdish aspirations for generations. Turkey has regularly massacred Kurds, destroyed their villages, extirpated their language and culture, even forbidden them to call themselves Kurds. The Kurdish separatist PKK, which launched an armed struggle against the Turkish state, has been brutally defeated by torture, kidnapping and mass murder. But these are the "bad Kurds," in the immortal words of the British novelist and ex-politician Jeffrey Archer, while those fighting an armed struggle against the regime in Baghdad are the "good Kurds."

Throughout the 1990s the Incerlik airbase in southwest Turkey was the scene of a situation so farcical that it still seems scarcely credible. British and American planes would take off to "protect" Iraqi Kurds in the mountains of northern Iraq, in the self-declared and wholly illegal "no-fly zones," while jets of the Turkish air force, often on the same day, would fly from the same base over the same mountains bombing the Turkish "bad Kurds," their flight paths frequently crossing.

Armed separatist rebellions are always put down by force. And civil wars are always the most brutal wars. The Union army literally set fire to the Confederate south in their crushing of the separatist forces in the American Civil war. The bigger the threat of the separatist rebels the greater will be the repression unless something happens—like the entry into the Albanian separatist struggle in Yugoslavia by the British and American air forces in the Kosovan civil war. Britain in Northern Ireland, Spain in the Basque country, India in the Punjab, Pakistan in Karachi, Nigeria in Biafra—the list is a long one.

Again the hypocritical insistence of Blair and Bush that the extreme violence in the civil war in Iraq was somehow unprecedented and warranted the much greater violence subsequently unleashed, is exposed by the most cursory examination of recent history.

Of course the initial pretext for the strangling of the children of Iraq by sanctions—infanticide masquerading as politics—was the regime's possession of weapons of mass destruction. Iraq, it turned out, by the end had no weapons of mass destruction. Not one weapon has been found in a country occupied not by a few hundred of Dr. Blix's inspectors, but by hundreds of thousands of foreign soldiers. The "Iraqi scientists," whom we were told were the key to finding weapons—which couldn't be done under the Blix inspections regime because their "minders" were intimidating them—are now all under the control of the occupiers. They are the minders now. Yet the only thing found so far is a single vial of Botox, twelve years old, found in a scientist's fridge. One vial of Botox—less than is carried in the ever-rosy cheeks of Joan Collins—is what, officially, we have to show for the war.

Of course simple logic shows that Bush and Blair must have known this all along—the only remotely plausible defense being that both men are idiots, fools rather than knaves. If Iraq truly had weapons of mass destruction it wouldn't have been invaded in the first place. Iraq was invaded not because it was dangerous to Britain and America but because it was *not* dangerous. North Korea will not be invaded precisely because it *is* dangerous.

If Iraq had weapons of mass destruction the invaders would have been absolutely petrified of looters finding them and spreading them around the region and the world to the highest bidder. As we all know they were not concerned about looters at all. If they thought that looters were carrying around those sort of weapons, the ones that could kill every human being in the world if splashed around efficiently enough, Bush and Blair would have been simply unable to sleep at night, lying in terror and stricken with panic at what might happen next. But they were not.

This brings me to my second and last meeting with Saddam Hussein.

During all my visits to Iraq between 1998 and 2002 I never asked to see Saddam and he never asked to see me. I was very content about that. At the time I thought he was being sensitive to my position in Britain by not inviting me for another public relations disaster. Later it emerged, in a book published in France, translated by the *Times* newspaper, and written by Saddam's longtime translator, Saman Abdul Majid, that in fact Saddam hated me. My very public pronouncement—that I was standing by the people of Iraq and not their president—was, said the author, a source of great irritation to him. He preferred the sycophants who endlessly praised and pledged their loyalty to him. Understandably this simple revelation about the real relationship between Saddam and me has had no great coverage in the British media.

But in August 2002 I asked to see Saddam Hussein. I did so because I wanted personally to appeal to him to allow the United Nations weapons inspectors to return to Iraq. I knew the reasons behind Iraq's previously less than trusting relations with a succession of inspections regimes. The British and American governments had undoubtedly strung out the work of the inspectors, constantly moving the goal posts, to keep the murderous sanctions in place. I knew, indeed I informed parliament, that previous inspectors, though nominally working for the UN, were in fact double agents, working also for the American and the Israeli governments. Though I was rubbished for saying so, it is now a given—and admitted by some of those involved. I knew, though they said differently in public, that Iraq was hoping to trade the return of inspectors for the lifting of sanctions and I supported that. This was summed up in Tariq Aziz's formulation after the savage bombardment of Iraq in the mangy and disreputable "Desert Fox" attack just before Ramadan and the run-up to Christmas 1998, an assault largely motivated by Bill Clinton's need to divert attention from the stain on Monica Lewinsky's blue dress.

"They can have sanctions, or they can have inspections. But they can't have both," said Aziz.

I knew also that even a climb down by Iraq and the re-admittance of the inspectors—whose withdrawal was ordered by Britain and America to facilitate the attack by the Desert Foxes (I wish I had a pound for every time I heard an ignorant journalist say that Iraq had "kicked out" the weapons inspectors)—might well not be enough to stop the clear and present danger of an American invasion. But I thought it was worth a try.

After what has happened I am sorry that I helped persuade the Iraqi regime to allow the inspectors to return. It is now clear beyond sane argument that Bush and Blair had long before decided to fall like the wolves of Sennacherib upon the people of Iraq whatever concessions the Iraqi leadership made. All that was achieved by the re-admittance of the inspectors was that Iraq proceeded to break up its conventional missile defenses before the approving eyes of the inspectors and most of the world, while British and American forces massed on their borders waiting for the order to invade. This was scheduled to occur once the UN window dressing had been arranged, but in the absence of that cover they would go in nakedly in defiance of international law. And of course, under the guise of weapons inspectors, Britain and America could infiltrate still more spies into Iraq, making the whole thing a ramp, a Trojan horse, for the coming attack.

So I asked Tariq Aziz for a meeting with Saddam Hussein. At this stage, with war apparently imminent, there was no telephone contact between the Iraqi leadership and Saddam. Just like in the days of Nebuchadnezzar it was all done with a word in the ear. Literally in a whisper, Aziz called in an official I had never seen before, presumably a "runner" working for Saddam. He whispered something in his ear and the man went off in a hurry. I think now that they might have thought I had brought some sort of secret message from the British, such was the alacrity with which the meeting was then arranged. This would not have been as strange as it seemed. I had informed the Iraqi leadership eighteen months before that the then British Middle East minister Peter Hain had asked me to set up a secret channel between him and the Iraqis.

Hain and I had met in a line in the voting lobby of the House of Commons—the strange archaic practice whereby every Member of Parliament must physically and immensely time-consumingly walk through a lobby to have their head counted to register their aye or no vote. One of the positive and indirectly democratic side effects of this system is that it sometimes provides the opportunity for backbenchers to buttonhole ministers on matters of concern. On this occasion, the minister, Peter Hain buttonholed me.

He began by asking me how things had been during my latest visit to Baghdad and Basra. Then he asked how the Iraqi leadership saw things developing. I asked him why he didn't ask the Iraqis that himself though, of course, I knew full well that all the channels of diplomatic communication had been closed tight. After all as the old war-leader Churchill himself was fond of saying, "Jaw-jaw is better than war-war." I said that I stood ready to be a go-between and suggested that he and I should open a secret channel between us, separate from our normal running battle conducted on the floor of the House.

"Let's take a walk," said Hain. We paced the library corridor, which runs parallel to the Commons chamber, and spoke to each other in quiet, almost whispered voices. He was nervous though I could tell excited about the possibilities.

"We will have to be *very* careful," he said. "Our intelligence services are *very* clever and very active. I can tell *you* that for certain." This I inferred was a none too thinly veiled warning that I was under security service surveillance. I expected as much. I have always said that while I have done and said many things I wouldn't want to appear on the front pages of the tabloid newspapers, I don't do and say things of which in my heart I am ashamed.

Hain and I parted having paced the corridor twice and having agreed to stay in touch, person to person, with not a word to anyone.

The next day I called upon the head of the Iraqi Interests Section, Dr. Mudhafar Amin, a graduate of Durham University, at the old Iraqi embassy building at 21 Queens Gate. I knew of course that phone conversations were impossible to keep secret and I had no confidence that the Iraqis had codes not already cracked by MI6. And I knew his embassy building was bugged, which was why he always kept his TV on, loudly, during many long, difficult conversations I had had with him. So I sat with him, writing notes about my conversation with Peter

Hain, notes which I carefully shredded later. He wrote me a note back saying that this was so potentially important that he should travel immediately to Baghdad with the news. He asked me to write out long-hand an account of the discussion and my recommendations as to how Baghdad should respond. This I did, adding the observation that Hain's comments about the intelligence services almost certainly meant that I was myself under observation, including telephone-tapping.

The next day Dr. Amin departed for Baghdad, via Jordan, carrying the sheets of paper written in my spidery hand.

He returned with the regime's answer: that I should actively encourage the opening of this channel with the minister and that I was hereby empowered to make the opening gambit I myself had suggested. This was a proposal that, without announcing it publicly, the British should cease to fly their "no-fly zone" sorties on Fridays—the Muslim holy day. In return the Iraqis would ensure perfect calm on those days in the zones, taking care to avoid anything which might be held to be a provocation. This confidence building measure, which would indicate that messages were being received understood and reciprocated, might lead to other more important gestures—like easing up on the highly restricted situation of Dr. Amin in London, balanced, say, with increased Iraqi measures to protect and rehabilitate the Church of St. George, the Anglican church next door to the Iraqi Ministry of Information, and so on.

Mr. Hain soon lost interest in this channel however, perhaps because this dialogue between the minister and Saddam through me came to be discovered by our *"very* active" security services or perhaps because Hain had overstepped his brief in a foreign office made increasingly redundant, as in Mrs. Thatcher's time, by the prime minister's propensity to conduct his own foreign policy on the telephone to Washington, or maybe for another reason. But somewhere in Baghdad, unless it wasn't treated with the same flame-resistant coating of some other documents, there exists in some bunker in some ministry, the evidence of an unlikely, eventually unfruitful ménage à trios: Saddam, Peter Hain and me.

And so, on my own journey to Baghdad in August 2002, I bore with me no good news for Saddam, only an extremely pessimistic analysis of the likelihood of war and my earnest plea on behalf of Dr. Blix's re-admittance.

It was an extraordinary meeting nonetheless. At the crack of dawn a smartly uniformed protocol officer banged on my hotel room door without prior notice and bade me to join him as quickly as possible. I was driven in a large black Mercedes with tinted windows and drawn black curtains. I had no idea where or even in which direction we were traveling. I was nervous in the car, thinking we'd make a pretty good target for an opportunist with a missile who reckoned they'd got some regime big-wig in their sights. We stopped five times, each time taking a break and another cup of horridly sweet tea in a succession of utterly anonymous buildings. I kept imagining the president was about to walk in and surprise us—but each time it was another car and on with the mystery tour.

Eventually we came to another unremarkable building, but this time we got into a high speed elevator that descended so deeply it made my ears pop. We arrived in a tastefully-lit room with curtained walls and banks of flowers artfully arranged. It didn't feel like the heart of darkness of the axis of evil. There, in a corner of the room, glancing shyly downwards as I walked towards him, was the most demonized man on the planet.

As had happened eight years before, Sadaam proffered a gentle handshake, strange from a man with a record of employing such an iron fist. With the aid of some classily deployed hair and moustache dye, a strict health regimen and, of course, no alcohol, Hussein didn't look much older, and perhaps even a little fitter, than the first time I'd met him.

The meeting was attended by all manner of flunkies, interpreters and even soldiers. Their nervousness contrasted sharply with Saddam's almost spooky Zen-like calm. A white-gloved orderly offered—in the twelfth year of UN sanctions—an array of Quality Street chocolates, the tin decorated with scenes of London. Saddam was clearly on a British-centered charm offensive.

Little cups of thick, sweet Turkish coffee appeared. The president was speaking. Protocol dictated that he took the first sip before other lesser mortals. I goofed, finishing mine before he even started. Pretending he hadn't noticed, Saddam invited me to begin sipping from a cup I'd already emptied.

The Iraqi strongman then regaled me with the

following anecdote, no doubt gleaned from his reading of war-time memoirs:

At the summit in Yalta, he said, Stalin, Roosevelt and Winston Churchill were at dinner when a goldfish in a large bowl of water was brought to the table. The three leaders were invited to use their cutlery to catch the fish. For the wily Stalin the fork was the weapon of choice. Stabbing repeatedly and vainly Stalin finally conceded defeat and passed the job to President Roosevelt.

Roosevelt tried with the knife, using its flat edge hoping to flick the fish out of the bowl. Again, exasperated, the American president had to give up.

At which point Churchill using his spoon slowly began emptying the bowl of the water until, bereft of oxygen, the fish finally succumbed.

"What became of the Britain of Winston Churchill?" Saddam asked.

In this anecdote the Iraqi leader displayed an exaggerated belief in the sophistication of British statecraft, at least as compared to the barbarous Russian and the brute "Roman" America, to which Saddam and many around the world believe Britain plays the role of "Greece," the older and wiser brother-empire.

If this belief is commonly found in the Arab world it is particularly prevalent in Iraq, despite Britain's role as former colonial power and co-tormentor in sanctions and war. Saddam Hussein put it in his own words during our meeting:

"You were a colonial power when the USA hadn't been invented," he said. "You were not hated like some others when you left your conquests and unlike those you should have been able to hold your heads up in front of your former subject peoples—but you seem determined to throw it all away."

"Take Iraq. Even at the height of our strategic relationship with the Soviet Union, Britain was the Iraqis' first choice. Whether for holidays—one million big-spending Iraqis a year used to travel to Britain—or for 'Made in Britain' goods."

"Our measurements, our scientific standards, our punctual double-decker buses, even our three-pin electric plugs were all based on the British," he continued.

"Our people trusted your banking system and have had their private savings seized and frozen. Iraqis, some of whom served you in the past, have died at the British embassy in Jordan waiting for visas to go to London."

"We will never understand why you have turned against us more than any other European country. If Britain had taken a more independent policy—one which took more account of your own interests and less of the interests of others—your country could have had a pre-eminent position in the Arab and Muslim world," said Saddam.

The Iraqi dictator, warming to his Churchillian theme, began to talk about the coming storm.

"If they come we are ready," he said. "We will fight them on the streets, from the rooftops, from house to house. We will never surrender our independence no matter what happens in any invasion.

"That is what Winston Churchill promised the invaders threatening England in 1940 and that is what we can promise the Crusader armies if they come here. Churchill and the British people meant what they promised Adolf Hitler. So do we. At the end, the Iraqi people do not love their country less than the British people love theirs.

"Iraq has never harmed Britain, nor its interests. In fact we were a very profitable part of Britain's in-

terests in the Arab world," said the man Tony Blair
insisted was within forty-five minutes of being able
to land chemical and biological weapons on British
heads in Cyprus.

Towards the end of what I felt had been an interesting though less than encouraging encounter I
requested a *tête-à-tête* discussion with Saddam. This is
diplomatic speak for indicating you have something
to say to the principals which you do not want to say
in front of the others. Saddam instantly dismissed
everyone from the room except Tariq Aziz, who
would henceforth translate the discussion between
us. Naji Sabri, the Iraqi foreign minister, got up to
leave with the others but Saddam motioned for him
to remain. The book written by the presidential in-
terpreter says that this private part of the meeting
lasted fifteen minutes. Here for the first time is what
happened:

Looking him straight in the eye I implied that
he had not been speaking the truth about Iraq's
weapons capability during our earlier discussion and
that he should stop grandstanding with me. I was
not there as a neutral, I was there as someone who
had given much of his political lifeblood to try and

help Iraq out of the terrible vise in which it was caught. I said that he should destroy any and all forbidden weapons systems and comply strictly with the demands of Dr. Blix. I was merely stating the obvious, though it will no doubt now be used against me. After all I said, once Iraq is out from under all this, the time will come when she can begin to build up her strength again.

Saddam gave me a direct look in return and this is exactly what he said:

"Mr. George. The Iraqi people owe you a lot. We are forever grateful for everything you have done to try to help us. I hear what you say and I know the sincerity with which you say it. I would not lie to you. So please hear me and believe me. *We do not have weapons of mass destruction.*"

At the time I was deeply despondent about this reply. In truth I did not believe him. I too had been deceived by the relentless barrage of propaganda, of so-called "intelligence" reports. Even I, a skeptic of skeptics of every statement of the British and American governments, had fallen for their lies. He must have *something,* I remember thinking to myself as he spoke.

As it turns out, the tyrant was telling the truth. And George Bush and Tony Blair, the self-appointed leaders of the civilized world, were the men whose pants were on fire.

My interview with Saddam Hussein, published in a British newspaper on August 11, 2002, created a sensation all around the world and in Iraq itself. My prediction, that by saying for the first time from his own mouth, "Iraq accepts and will implement all UN resolutions," Saddam had implicitly agreed to allow Dr. Blix to bring his arms inspectors in, was widely ridiculed. I was traduced as a mouthpiece for Saddam all over again. But it was true—he did subsequently allow them back in. And a fat lot of good it did him.

My plea for those inspectors to be given more time would later be rubbished in the same way. But if they had been given longer, we would not now be in the mess we're in. CNN demanded further and better particulars of where exactly the meeting had taken place. They didn't like my answer that even if I knew I wouldn't tell them because the details could only make it easier for Bush to assassinate the Iraqi leader and I didn't approve of killing other people's presidents. Experts tried to work out how far underground we must have been for the elevator journey to have taken as long as it did, though I think they were overestimating the efficiency of Iraqi lifts after twelve years of sanctions. Information minister Mohammed Saeed al-Sahhaf—later known as "Comical Ali"—was not quite up to speed when he denounced my statements about allowing arms inspectors to return, saying "the era of arms inspections in Iraq is over." Saddam himself was furious about my description of the cloak and dagger nature of the meeting and the picture it painted of him skulking underground. The Iraqis put out a statement that the meeting had taken place in a presidential palace. If only all presidential palaces had been so modest.

So that is the story of Saddam and me. Not much of a story really, certainly not the relationship the British government has tried so desperately to portray. Three separate sets of documents placing me in the pay of the Saddam regime emerged from the ashes after the fall of Baghdad. The Pulitzer prize-winning *Christian Science Monitor* bought documents that purported to show me receiving $10 million in cash from a son of Saddam whom I'd never met, starting before I had ever set foot in Iraq (and before the son in question had any role in the regime) and finishing after I had visited Iraq for the last time, including a $1 million payment on a given date when I was in fact online to readers of the *Guardian* newspaper from my office in the House of Commons. These documents were purchased (though the newspaper says they did not know that the freelance reporter who wrote their story, Philip Smucker, essentially paid for them) from a retired Iraqi general who later sold a second set of documents to the British newspaper the *Mail on Sunday,* which claimed payments to me of more millions from Saddam's other son. When the *Mail on Sunday* subjected their documents to forensic examination, their expert, Dr. Audrey Giles, former head of the questioned-documents section of Scotland Yard's forensic science laboratory, found them to be forgeries.

Following the *Mail on Sunday's* revelations, the *Christian Science Monitor* began to examine forensically the documents on which they had based their claim. By testing the age of the paper and ink they quickly established that the documents purporting to have been written in 1992 and the documents allegedly written eleven years later had, in fact, been written at the same time. These, too, were declared forgeries. Having published an apology and accepted full responsibility, the *Christian Science Monitor* would later pay me substantial damages and costs and make a statement of contrition in the High Court in London.

In December 2003 judgment was delivered in the High Court in London on another set of documents that made allegations about me, this time employed by the *Daily Telegraph* newspaper to assert that I was in the pay of Saddam Hussein. The judge, Mr. Justice Eady, administered a severe judicial caning to the *Telegraph,* awarding me $280,000, and costs estimated at over $2 million. The newspaper has now appealed against the judgment and a hearing is pending. So I haven't even received one penny piece as yet in damages.

Allegations flowed freely: The robotic Tory MP Andrew Robathan, who'd fought in the first attack on Iraq in 1991, called for an investigation into a claim that I had received "one million barrels of oil" from Saddam which he said would be worth $37 million. In January of 2004 an Iraqi newspaper linked to Ahmed Chalabi said that, in fact, I had received 19 million barrels of oil—by Robathan's calculations, therefore, almost $1 billion.

All of these allegations are baseless. The truth is neither Saddam Hussein nor anyone else in Iraq ever gave me a cent, though the newspapers who made false claims are going to have to pay me a pretty penny.

I have never met any official of the Iraqi oil ministry nor ever visited the ministry itself. I have never seen a barrel of oil (apart from one rolled to my doorstep by an English tabloid newspaper), owned one, bought or sold one. Neither has anyone else on my behalf. My stand with the people of Iraq was a labor of love. That's the kind of labor the bank robber Chalabi and the gutter-snipes of the right-wing press simply cannot understand.

All that remains is for me draw up a political balance sheet about the Iraqi dictator. Saddam Hussein was a Third World dictator of a kind that was common around the world in the Cold War years and is slowly but surely dying out or being done to death. He was not Hitler. Hitler was the all-powerful dictator of a powerful, technologically advanced country at the heart of Europe who intended to rule

the entire world and who in an industrialized geno-
cide massacred more than six million Jews as well as
countless communists, Gypsies, homosexuals, disabled people and occupied peoples of all kinds. Saddam, in contrast, had only regional ambitions and all
of them had failed utterly, well over a decade before
the wholly unnecessary invasion and occupation of
his country. Saddam was a ruthless and cruel man
who thought little about signing the death warrants
of even close comrades and still less about ordering
the merciless crushing of potential threats to his
regime. In that he was little different to the leaders of
most regimes; regime survival is the ultimate prior-
ity of most systems—we just don't know it in our
own countries, yet.

It was not a dishonorable thing for an Arab ruler
to aspire to military might. Iraq is surrounded by
dangerous neighbors who have designs upon it or
wish to see it disappear. Turkey, Iran and Israel are all
militarily powerful and all of them have or have
been trying to acquire weapons of mass destruction.
In any case the mere possession of WMD is not of
itself a threat; it can even help keep the peace. Isn't
that the rationale behind our own possession of nuclear weapons? When the USSR acquired its nuclear

bomb to balance that of the Americans we were always told that this mutually assured destruction equation was the reason for Europe's longest period of peace.

Unless you are a partisan who believes that the Zionist state should have nuclear weapons while the Arabs whose land it has taken should be broken and destroyed if they try to balance Israeli power, it must be accepted—in the absence of international intervention to obtain justice—that an Arab ruler worth his salt will seek to strike that balance. The same is true as regards Turkey, which covets Mosul and oil-rich Kirkuk in Iraq. And of course with the Persian power to the east.

Saddam Hussein committed two gigantic miscalculations, either one of which, had there been any democracy at all in Iraq, would have been his downfall long ago. I refer to the invasion of Iran, at the behest of the West, and the invasion of Kuwait in defiance of it.

By the standards of dictatorships Saddam himself may have been a killer but he was not a thief. He virtually never traveled overseas and owned no properties or wealth abroad. What good would it have done him? He knew that he would either die, still the all-powerful president of a rich country, or be brought down with a violent crash with no hiding place overseas. The same could not be said of his grasping family, and their orgy of violence and pillaging of the country's wealth played a decisive role in fatally weakening the regime from within.

By all accounts Saddam Hussein was a generous friend as well as a deadly enemy, sometimes at one and the same time. He sent one party opponent—with whom he'd been classmates—to the Iraqi mission at the UN in New York. He told him, "you have to leave the country or our dispute will turn dangerous for you." Whilst in New York the man was constantly on the telephone asking Saddam for ever more generous spending permissions, on one occasion asking for jewelry his wife had fancied on a visit to Tiffany. Saddam loved this man and gave him everything. Yet when he returned from the UN to Baghdad and Saddam suspected him of plotting against him, he personally killed him.

At a time when human rights has become an international phenomenon it was easy for the likes of Bush and Blair, hypocrites both, to demonize a regime as careless of such basic human rights as that of Saddam. But that was not the real reason Iraq was crushed. In truth since the 1916 Sykes-Picot partition of the Ottoman empire, it has been an article of faith of imperialism to keep the Arab world divided and weak.

Just as Stalin industrialized the Soviet Union, so Saddam piloted Iraq's "Great Leap Forward." In fact his best days were when he was vice-president before he got the top job. He pioneered the nationalization of the oil industry, the revenues of which, unlike other Arab countries, were re-invested in the country and its people. The West prefers its petro-dollars recycled into the bordellos, casinos, stock exchanges and property markets of the Occident.

Iraq built the best health service in the Middle East, and made huge advances in the education sector—sending vast numbers of students to the West for post-graduate studies and technical training. My first ever exposure to Iraqis was in the early seventies when their handsome and prosperous-looking students from the air training school in Scone in Perthshire, Scotland used to take all the prettiest girls on our local dance-floors. They may well have been pleased to be in Dundee, but those were large rolls of dinars in their pockets, courtesy of their country's oil wealth.

The very fact that there could be such a hulla-baloo about weapons inspectors interviewing Iraqi scientists depended on Iraq, an Arab Third-World country, having a science base in the first place. This dwarfed all other Arab countries, and of course in the other oil-rich lands most people with scientific and technical expertise were simply hired as expatri-ate labor from abroad.

In short, Saddam had some significant achieve-ments, and Iraq at first benefited more than it suf-fered from his rule. But he committed two gigantic mistakes in invading Iran and Kuwait, for which his country paid severely. Yet Saddam himself didn't pay as he should have done, with his political life. He managed to keep his country together until 1991 when the West facilitated the severance, which will become final in the years to come, of Kurdistan. In-deed he is likely to have been the leader in history who came closest to creating a truly Iraqi national identity, and he developed Iraq and the living, health, social and educational standards of his peo-ple. But the brutality of his regime and the sheer lack of democracy meant that he could in the end be iso-lated and defeated. Democracy is not a panacea and the benefits of its Westminster model are often oversold in relation to Third World countries. But in a crew of yes-men, where no one can tell the ruler he's wrong without paying with his head, the ship only needs to set a course that's out by an inch. Before long it is adrift and lost.

It should be noted that the majority of Arabs and Muslims in the world would not agree with my balance sheet—which ultimately declares Saddam bankrupt. As far as they are concerned, the good he did, perhaps more importantly the defiance he represented, was more important than the many debits. They take a look around at their own puppet presidents and corrupt royals and then they look at Saddam Hussein. For them, in the land of the blind the one-eyed man is king.

MR. GALLOWAY GOES TO WASHINGTON

It was on the morning of Thursday, May 12, 2005 that I decided it was time to go to Washington. On that day, the much-trailed Senate Homeland Security sub-committee report finally appeared. As expected, it named me as having received allocations for 20 million barrels of oil, which at the time was valued at around $500 million. If it hadn't been so fantastical, the idea would have been very worrisome. This particular allegation—and sometimes it's difficult to keep track of what I'm supposed to have received and from whom!—had been swimming about for months, so I wasn't too surprised to find it in the report. Nor was I surprised that the report failed to include any of the dozens of American companies and individuals allegedly involved in oil deals with Iraq. A blackout of their names had been imposed by the U.S. government lest, presumably, the trail led too closely to members of the Bush administration. The omitted are likely to include some of the 270 names that the convicted fraudster, and then Iraqi oil supremo, Ahmed Chalabi claimed had been found in the oil ministry in Baghdad after the invasion. Chalabi's ignominious exit from Jordan has clearly done nothing to curb his interest in intrigue.

The Senate report had been embargoed until the early hours of the morning, giving the news agencies and international media plenty of time to prepare their copy. My friend Ron McKay fielded dozens of calls, explaining that there was nothing new in the report, that it was basically the same material the Duelfer report (a CIA-commissioned inquiry based on the work of the Iraq Survey Group) had produced months before, and that I not only categorically denied having any part in oil trades but had not even been given the opportunity to put that denial before the committee, despite having written to its chair asking for the opportunity to do so. It was summary injustice. I had been convicted in absentia, without being able to put a defense to the partisan group of 13 senators. As I said to the media, even in Kafka some kind of defense was allowed.

Ron put out a brief statement on my behalf: "It's Groundhog Day again. These are the same false allegations that are still the subject of a libel action with the *Daily Telegraph* (so far I'm £1.6million [nearly $3 million] up). This is a lickspittle Republican committee, acting on the wishes of George W. Bush. Isn't it strange—and contrary to natural justice you might think—that I have written and emailed repeatedly asking for the opportunity to appear before the committee to provide evidence and rebut their assumptions and they have yet to respond, while apparently making a judgment? Why am I not surprised? Let me repeat. I have never traded in a barrel of oil, or any vouchers for it. I have never seen a barrel of oil apart from the one the *Sun* newspaper deposited in my front garden. And no one has acted on my behalf, trading in oil—Middle Eastern, olive, patchouli or any other—or in vouchers, whatever they are.

The reference to the Murdoch-owned tabloid newspaper, which never knowingly lets the facts get in the way of a monstering, resulted from an incident when its reporters rolled a barrel of oil into my front garden in south London in the early hours of the morning. The Duelfer report had just appeared and they wanted to get a photograph of me wrestling with the barrel. This is what passes for news reportage in Britain's top-selling daily.

When the story broke, I was in my house in Portugal (incidentally, it's hardly a hacienda as has been alleged in much of the media, and it has a 100 percent, $150,000 mortgage on it). I called Ron at his home in Scotland early in the morning, to see how the story was playing at home. Massively, was the answer. It was leading the news programs as well as being plastered over all of the newspapers.

The two of us had more than once before discussed whether, despite not having received an invitation, I should just turn up at the committee in Washington and demand a hearing. We had decided to let it go, assuming that there would be a formal invitation before any damning judgment was delivered.

But now, as the rain battered down on my terrace outside, I asked Ron again what he thought of a transatlantic trip. "I think it's time to go to Washington," he replied.

The phone lines sizzled all day as the story developed momentum. British Washington correspondents caught up with the committee's Republican chairman, Norm Coleman, and its ranking Democrat Carl Levin, and asked if I had, indeed, contacted the judgmental Senators. "Not even by carrier pigeon," said Coleman, who then extended an invitation to me through the international media. There "would be a seat for Galloway" the following Tuesday to put his case.

Watching this, through my satellite system, at the center of a media maelstrom, I could only shake my head in disbelief. It was as if this was happening to someone else, some curiously familiar doppelganger. I wondered what my bank manager might be thinking, the one who held my considerable overdraft, or the credit card companies, almost all of who had withdrawn my credit. A Member of Parliament's salary is just over $100,000 a year and, in addition, I write a well-paid column for a Sunday newspaper. But I employ more assistants and researchers than my parliamentary budget allows for and I travel, without expenses, all over the country to give speeches—by my accounting nearly 1,200 since 9/11. While my lifestyle is comfortable it's hardly exotic. I don't drink, and Havana cigars together with the occasional suit from Hugo Boss are my sole extravagances. Since being elected in May as the new MP for Bethnal Green and Bow my outlays had increased. I'd had to rent an apartment in the constituency and set up a local office. I could hardly plead poverty but when I looked at what I was supposed to be worth through oil tradings, and watched the news clips and pundits pontificate, I could only give a wry chuckle.

I might have left well alone and waited for the storm to die out. But not even my bitterest enemies, and there are quite a few, could accuse me of running away from a fight. So, the decision was confirmed. I was off to Washington. And I was beginning to relish it.

I was to be accompanied by Ron, who would deal with the press, and by my political assistant Asad Rehman. It fell to Asad to set up the arrangements, the flights and hotel booking, selecting the promisingly-named President Inn on the internet. "It was about the only one we could afford," he recalls, "about $75 a night, whereas the downtown prices were astronomical, up to $800 dollars." He said it looked OK on the website. How deceptive internet photographs can be!

I was footing the bill. An inquiry to the committee about whether any expenses would be paid was brusquely and immediately rebuffed. The flights, the cheapest we could arrange at the last minute, were booked on KLM, with a plane change in Amsterdam. The outward journey left London at 8:00 am on the Monday morning. Ron and I, after bedding down in my constituency home in Cheshire Street, were up just after 5:00 am, neither having slept particularly well. We drove to the airport in my big blue Mercedes, bought third-hand 10 years ago from fellow Scottish MP Jimmy Wray, who is supplier of all manner of interesting goods and gee-gaws to her majesty's government, backbenchers and opposition. Asad was being picked up by the redoubtable Mohammad Zabadne, who not only acted as chauffeur but had persuaded three hijab-wearing family members to come along too, dragooning them into holding up home-made banners of support for me to the media.

And they were there in plenty at Heathrow's Terminal Four, rushing up in a tangle of cameras and cables to me and Ron as we walked towards check-in. It was to be the first of many scrums that day. A Scottish Television reporter, David Cowan, had booked himself on the same flight and a BBC Scotland cameraman was also on the plane. Reluctantly I had agreed to brief in-flight interviews, if the plane's captain was amenable. When Ron and I walked into the terminal building, with Rehman and the Zabadne clan not far behind, another media maul broke out as the crews and reporters without accreditation from the airport were barred from following us.

Occasionally, being an MP, even one as hounded as I am, has its benefits. We managed to wangle upgrades to business class, but the standard was poor—there might have been additional legroom, but the food was almost inedible. Fortunately I am able to drop off to sleep easily, a skill acquired after many years of exhausting practice on some of the world's most inhospitable modes of transport. Asad followed my lead, though he required the assistance of what looked like a highwayman's mask pulled down over his eyes.

I woke before we touched down in Amsterdam, where we took a two-hour prowl around the airport. Then it was onto another KLM plane for the hike across the Pond. We were expecting lengthy questioning by immigration at Washington's Dulles Airport but, including the now mandatory fingerprints and eye scans, it took minutes rather than hours. A preconception pleasantly disproved.

But if I had thought that we could slip quietly into the United States, I was rapidly disabused. Another press posse awaited us on the concourse. I counted 12 television cameras and at least 15 reporters with thrusting microphones. Among the journalists, his head towering above the crowd, was my old friend Bob Wylie from BBC Scotland, who had arrived a day earlier. Sky TV's Glen Oglaza had caught an earlier, direct flight from London and was also prominent.

I don't generally prepare speeches in advance or speak from notes but there was one line I was determined to deliver. Echoing the words of the great Scottish socialist and teacher John Maclean at his First World War trial for sedition I said, "I come here not as the accused but as the accuser." Maclean was jailed and then freed by popular acclaim. That was a parallel too far!

The President Inn, in the north east of Washington, proved less than presidential. A knot of drunks and panhandlers appeared to be in permanent session round the entrance, and our taxi driver warned,

"Don't go out at night around here. You'll get shot!" Welcome to the capital of the world's superpower.

As well as the Senate investigation into the oil-for-food program, there was a parallel investigation underway by the United Nations. Neither operation was willing to share its information with the other. The Senate committee was openly opposed to the United Nations and all of its works, while the UN was clearly unwilling to provide any potential ammunition for its own destruction. That's geopolitics. The UN inquiry, through Ron, had asked to talk to me in advance of my appearance at the committee. I had agreed. After all, I had nothing to hide, and I thought it might be a useful rehearsal for the main event in front of the Senate the following day.

Two youthful UN counsels (it's not just the police who appear younger as you get older!) turned up at the hotel for the interview which, not so much for security reasons but because the hotel had no proper lobby in which to hold it, took place in Ron's bedroom. The two counsels, one American and one Briton, were particularly interested in the successful Jordanian businessman, Fawaz Zureikat. I had been introduced to Fawaz by my wife, Amineh Abu-Zayyad, who knew him from her time studying in Jordan. Zureikat was, independently of me, a vigorous anti-sanctions campaigner. Indeed, how could he not be when under sanctions at least a million Iraqis died, the majority of them children? Undoubtedly Saddam worked to bypass sanctions—this was the main contention of the Senate committee— but it makes my blood boil when my critics claim that the sanctions regime, if properly observed, could have fed and nurtured the Iraqi populace. What Iraq was allowed to sell under the program amounted to less than 40 cents a person, and this was supposed to be sufficient not only for food and housing but for the entire infrastructure of the country. I was in Iraq many times during sanctions and witnessed not only the almost total breakdown of a once hugely wealthy society but a mass collective punishment, allegedly outlawed under Geneva conventions, which murdered hundreds of thousands of innocent men, women and children.

I became fast friends with Fawaz and was best man at his wedding. The suave, sophisticated Jordanian, with impeccable English and the manners to boot, became chairman of the Mariam Appeal, the organization I had set up to help the then four-year-old leukemia sufferer, Mariam Hamza, who I discovered on the point of death in a cancer ward in Baghdad. We decided to bring her to Britain to try to save her life and to advertise the case against sanctions. England's most famous and best-regarded cancer hospital refused to take her, so we got her admitted to the Sick Children's Hospital in Glasgow, which was in my constituency. The bill for her hospital treatment during her seven-month stay came to over £70,000 ($100,000), which I had pledged to pay.

There had never been any intention to register the Mariam Appeal as a charity because charities, according to English law, cannot campaign politically. And the appeal was nothing if not highly and flamboyantly political. Among other successful publicity wheezes, it was responsible for projecting a big antiwar slogan onto the Houses of Parliament at night, a story that made the front pages of the *Guardian* and *Daily Mirror* newspapers. We also broke sanctions, and risked imprisonment, by flying a plane into Iraq when the whole country was a no-fly zone. And we organised the Big Ben to Baghdad trip, a crowd of us taking an aged London double-decker Routemaster bus all the way to Iraq in order to publicize the anti-sanctions cause.

But despite the fact that the Mariam fund was evidently engaged in prominent political campaigning, an inquiry was launched by the Attorney General, Lord Goldsmith, to establish if it should, in fact, have been registered as a charity. The noble lord is one of Prime Minister Tony Blair's best friends and I judged, correctly I'm sure, that this was another politically-inspired move to publicly blackguard me. The outcome was a curious compromise, a typically British fudge. The Charity Commission ruled that for the medical relief work it undertook, the Mariam Appeal should have been registered as a charity, while for its political work it should not. Make sense of that. The two aims were obviously indivisible, though evidently not to the commissioners. In any event, the commissioners' final report, having had access to all the appeal's bank statements, acquitted the campaign of any financial impropriety and ruled that the monies raised had been properly used. It was ironic, surely, that almost none of the cash raised had come from British citizens—and certainly none of the donors had complained!—but here was an august, thoroughly British institution, passing judgment.

Fawaz Zureikat had, in several tranches, donated

around £375,000 to the campaign. Other major donors included the president of the United Arab Emirates and the Saudi crown prince, which was remarkable given that I had been openly hostile to the Saudi monarchy for many years. It just showed how leading figures in the Arab world regarded sanctions. It was Zureikat's donation that the two UN investigators were most interested in, however; specifically, they wanted to know its provenance.

I replied wearily to their line of questioning—I intended to be considerably more forceful the following day—because I had answered the questions many times before. Fawaz, I replied, was a successful businessman trading with Iraq before I knew him. I didn't ask him how he made his money or how much, any more than I would ask anyone else. I learned later, much later, when all of this started to come out, that he was, apparently, trading in oil. But that was only a small part of his business in Iraq—he was also involved in major engineering and infrastructural projects, including the equipping of Baghdad airport.

I went on to point out that he was an agent for a variety of international companies, including the French company Thomson, and that he also did business in many other Middle Eastern and former Eastern Bloc countries.

The allegation, which would become clearer next day, was that Zureikat had been my conduit, acting for me in uplifting and marketing 20 million barrels of oil, and that he had, also on my behalf, been paying illegal kickbacks to the regime. The latter was an assumption, based on documents allegedly recovered from the oil ministry in Baghdad. To support the former, all that the committee had was my name on four foolscap pages referring to four oil "deals." There were no witnesses, no reliable supporting documents, in fact not a shred of evidence to establish that any of this had happened.

The two investigators said that they were anxious to talk to Zureikat. I said that I would try to pass on the message but reminded them that, immediately prior to the invasion and occupation of Iraq, Fawaz had been arrested by the Jordanian authorities, almost certainly at the behest of the U.S., and had been interrogated for 27 days. There couldn't be very much about Fawaz that wasn't already known, I added. The senior counsel, Mark Califano, responded, "I'm not sure the Jordanians are too anxious to be helpful to our inquiry."

That was hardly surprising. Jordan, along with Turkey, was the major beneficiary of the massive and illegal oil smuggling operation which kept both countries economies afloat throughout the 10 years of sanctions. Smuggling is perhaps the wrong description because, although what passed was illegal, the trucks carrying the oil were allowed to pass freely and openly, without interdiction by the United States and the United Nations inspectors on the borders. This was done to keep the support of both countries for the "coalition" against Iraq. Real politick, hypocrisy—is there any difference? Naturally I would point this out on the morrow.

It was evening in Washington when the two UN investigators left. The three of us—Ron, Asad and myself—were guests at a dinner hosted by Bob Wylie and the BBC in a smart downtown restaurant. On the taxi ride home we booked the stoical driver for a 7:30 am pick-up the next morning to take us down to the Capitol where the hearing was to be held. "Just don't go out on your own at night around here," were the driver's last words, as he put the car into gear. The three of us looked at each other and finished the warning. "Or you'll get shot!"

I was awake at 3:30 am and up shortly after that.

I felt tired, but well prepared, because I had been over the terrain so many times before. I was even looking forward to the Senate appearance, relishing the opportunity to relate to the American people, through this televised event, much of what I had been saying on the anti-war stump for the previous two years. I would dismiss the oil allegations because I knew they had no foundation in fact. I wasn't in Washington to defend myself, but to attack the Bush administration and the criminal foreign policy which had led to the invasion and its brutal aftermath.

Asad and Ron were in the hotel lobby waiting for the taxi when I came out of the lift.

I had already phoned my chum Seumas Milne on the *Guardian* in London, and learned that the day's news was dominated, once again, by fallout from Iraq. The paper's lead story provided apposite material for what I was going to say to the Senators. The British charity Christian Aid was claiming that at least $20 billion in oil revenues and other Iraqi funds intended to rebuild the country had disappeared from banks administered by the Coalition Provisional Authority, the U.S. administration of the country. Where the money had gone was a mystery. Christian Aid compared the absence of facts and accountability over these huge Iraqi oil revenues to the abundant information on the $18.4 billion of U.S. taxpayer' contributions presently being spent in Iraq. No less than four separate audits of the funds were underway. Christian Aid called on the Treasury Department, the U.S. agency responsible for pushing Iraq to privatize its economy—and before that, for confiscating billions of dollars in Iraqi assets worldwide—and the CPA to come out publicly with transparent figures.

As the three of us traveled towards the center of Washington in the building traffic we talked, once again, about the kind of approach I should take with the committee, the temper of my speech. Not anger and hostility, we all agreed, but a steely, withering contempt. As a former boxer I thought of it this way: I must be neither Mohammed Ali nor Mike Tyson; I must aim for Rocky Marciano. Remorseless. Blow after blow after blow. Controlled aggression. It wouldn't quite work out that way.

I had agreed to meet up prior to the hearing with the BBC's Washington correspondent, Clive Myrie, and to call him when we had located a coffee shop where an interview could take place. The taxi dropped us at the back of the Everett Dirksen building where the committee was meeting. Asad had wanted a traditional American diner breakfast, but all we could find was an upmarket delicatessen. We had to make do with bagels but the coffee was excellent. As I picked at my food Ron and Asad were being blitzed by telephone calls and had to walk off some distance to avoid their conversations interfering with the TV sound. The Scottish TV reporter David Calder and his cameraman had turned up and were filming the BBC filming me.

Through this rather surreal, early-morning tableau people on their way to work climbed the stairs to the deli and lined up for their breakfasts. Asad briefly disappeared searching for an internet connection, then returned. I finished the Myrie interview and a second cup of coffee, stood up and said, "Right. Shall we?"

Ron later wrote, "It seemed like a bright Washington movie-set morning as we walked towards the building." It was. We had become characters in a film. We did not know it but we were approaching the Dirksen building from the rear and we had to ask directions to the main entrance. As we turned around the first corner we were immediately spotted by a waiting press pack, bristling with microphones and video cameras. They began a charge down the side-walk towards us. The first question, from a young British woman TV reporter was: "Do you think you'll be a free man tonight, Mr. Galloway?"

"I expected a director to shout: 'Cut. That's a take. And print it!' " Ron observed later.

An impromptu press conference broke out as we tried to make our way around to the front of the building. The questions were rapid-fire but pre-dictable. As I did my best to answer them I caught sight of a familiar figure, clutching, somewhat bizarrely, a half-chewed banana. He was more cor-pulent than the last time I had met him and now sported a beard but I instantly recognized Christo-pher Hitchens, an old adversary and former leftie now lucratively renounced of his past and plying his journalistic trade in the service of those promoting the war. Hitchens, together with another bearded reporter from the Washington-based *New Republic,* seemed primarily interested in whether I could prove that I had asked to be invited to the commit-tee. I have had little time for the noted imbiber, since the time he sold out the Palestinian cause, certainly long before he backed the war and damned people like me who had opposed it.

Hitchens became increasingly apoplectic as I declined to answer his shouted questions. "Tell us about the suicide-murderers, Mr. Galloway, that your friend Saddam was paying for," he yelled. It was depressing to recognize the lexicon of Ariel Sharon coming from the mouth of someone who was once counted among Britain's brightest left-wing stars.

"Christopher, your hands are shaking," I bellowed back to him over the heads of the pressing reporters. "Go and have another drink." It was, after all, approaching 9:00 in the morning. Hitchens continued his asides about whether I had actually written to the committee as we passed through security and the x-ray machine and into the cavernous building. I had had enough. In front of the clicking cameras and whirring tapes I turned around and let him have it: "You are a drink-sodden, former Trotskyite popinjay," I shouted; at which point Hitchens slid away from the gathering muttering, "You thug."

The Senate building was extremely grand, with long wide corridors punctuated by little roped-off media corrals where TV cameras would grab passing senators for their comments. Inside room 106, which seemed large enough to hold a soccer field, dozens of reporters and media crews were already in place. Along one wall print journalists with laptops fired up were preparing their articles. Facing them were TV cameras and personnel. In the center of the room was seating for around 300 people on chairs that faced the long dais where the senators would sit. The senators' aides and legal counsels were already gathering. Immediately in front of the dais was a table, with three chairs and individual microphones, where the witnesses would take their places. It was a scene unlike anything I had ever encountered inside the rather staid and tradition-bound House of Commons and I found it immensely refreshing.

The media hubbub was continuing as Asad, Ron and I took seats half a dozen rows back in the spectator section. Questions were being fired, reporters pushed each other and fought for space in the gangway between two banks of seating. It was difficult not to be caught up in the mounting excitement, although mentally I was rehearsing what I would say when summoned.

I was the second witness to be called. The first, or rather the first three, were Senate counsels who, in labyrinthine detail, outlined the case against

Texas-based Bayoil, an American company that had apparently banked shedloads of profits from trading in Iraqi oil and kicked back millions of dollars to the regime. Why this company was being singled out for attention, rather than approximately 268 other companies and individuals who had allegedly done the same thing, was not obvious to me. These witnesses were treated in a friendly fashion by the three Senators sitting on the top bench, with more than a dozen aides behind them.

I was forming an initial impression of Norm Coleman, the chairman. He is a lean man in his early fifties but looks younger. He evidently pays considerable attention to his appearance, and has a full head of hair, elaborately coifed. He talked in a bored monotone, without color in his declamations, dryly teeing up each response. He has flitted across the political spectrum in pursuit of opportunity, from student opponent of Richard Nixon, through card-carrying Democratic Party membership, to becoming a right-wing Minnesota Republican. His Senate election victory was only ensured when his incumbent opponent, Paul Wellstone, perished in a plane crash less than two weeks before the election. He has been spoken of as a potential presidential candidate. For the front desk of the President Inn, I thought as he droned on, certainly no higher.

What seemed like an exercise in somnolence turned to high farce half an hour into the preceding testimony. I needed to be prepared and, as Mr. Churchill put it, never pass up the opportunity of a precautionary pee. I whispered to Ron, "Do you know where the toilet is?" He gave a follow-me gesture and rose. As both of us walked into the wide corridor towards the nearest bathroom we realized that we had trailed half the attendant media posse in our slipstream. It reminded me of a famous TV incident where Helen Liddell, now the British Governor-General to Australia, but then an aide to the businessman and crook Robert Maxwell, was filmed following her boss into the men's bathroom at the Edinburgh Commonwealth Games.

When we returned, much better prepared, the first act were still outlining the methods that Bayoil had employed to illegally import millions of gallons of oil and give millions of dollars in kickbacks to the Hussein regime. Iraq had introduced a system where oil companies had to pay a tithe, typically 10 cents a barrel, on oil they lifted from the country. This was in breach of UN sanctions laws. The irony was, and not for the first time, that Bayoil had been breaking the law to import oil to feed the insatiable US market.

As the counsels' testimony proceeded, a female committee worker handed me a large file of papers relating to the day's business. Asad and Ron fell on them and began tearing out relevant pages. All of these productions, apparently proofs positive, were to be flashed up on screens to the court and attendant media.

We three Brits were surprised that only three of the 13 Senators on the committee, seven Republicans and six Democrats, had turned up for the hearing, and this was to drop to two, Norm Coleman and Carl Levin, when I was called. The excuse, apparently, was pressure of business elsewhere. Perhaps the others had been better briefed about me than the remaining double act. But two out of 13! Have they never heard of a quorum? That's something else you wouldn't get away with in the Mother of Parliaments.

Eventually the Three Stooges were dismissed. Before I was called, Senator Coleman launched into a lengthy accusatory preamble, citing my alleged misdemeanors and felonies. I couldn't help but thinking, as my dander rose, that Coleman was regarding this as a career-making opportunity, to be captured forever on television like the grainy footage of his old nemesis, Richard Nixon, and his assault on Alger Hiss. If that was indeed the case it was very, very poor judgment on his part.

As Coleman read out the allegations, or rather the conclusions the committee had come to, I became more and more angry. This was like the verdict being delivered in a show trial, although I hadn't even been allowed to attend the proceedings. Asad and Ron both whispered in my ear. The gist of their comments was "forget the statesmanlike approach, go for him."

Finally I was called to testify. I sat down in the middle seat at the table, which was deliberately set at a lower elevation than the Senators' lofty perches. Asad sat on my right, Ron on my left, in front of three microphones. It had been agreed that I would have 10 minutes to make a statement before being questioned. Asad scribbled a note and passed it to Ron. "Don't forget the mics are live." Ron nodded.

Ron had already pulled out the five documents that allegedly "incriminated" me, four seeming to contain details of oil deals, the fifth a letter I had written giving Fawaz Zureikat the authority to deal with matters relating to the Mariam Appeal in Iraq. It was one of the committee's charges that the appeal had benefited in petrodollars by this, or rather that this was a way of concealing the fact that I was the beneficiary. The report which the committee had issued days earlier didn't say that I had actually pocketed any cash—it was legalistically drafted simply to lead readers to this conclusion—but that I had been given oil allocations and these had been taken up by Zureikat, on my behalf. But hours before this appearance Coleman would openly allege, on Channel 4 and in the *Times* and *Daily Telegraph* newspapers, that I had done so, and handsomely. Writs to follow, guys.

The crucial documents, the virtual totality of the case, which were flashed up on a large screen, purported to be original papers from the oil ministry in Baghdad, one of the few government buildings to be protected from looting by American troops. They even appeared to include blacked-out signatures. But it soon became clear that the documents were not the originals but were instead mock ups. Ron was later to tell me that, when he had first seen them, in the file handed out by the committee before the proceedings started, he had felt a surge of alarm. The versions here, although they referred to the same oil deals and claimed to be the same documents as those uncovered by the Duelfer inquiry, were, in fact, quite different. The Duelfer versions contained a crude forgery of my name, whereas these did not. Furthermore, the documents were in English, rather than Arabic. It didn't make sense that one Iraqi government department would communicate to another in English. Having seen real Iraq government documents Ron also noticed that the official stamp, which always embellished state documents, was missing from those on display at the committee. We realized that these grandly-titled "exhibits" were not original documents at all but merely translations of those allegedly found in the oil ministry in Baghdad. Nowhere in the huge file circulated by the committee was this made clear. Almost totally obscured on the photocopied pages by these U.S.-produced sheets were what I described as "gray smudges." Barely discernible through the blur were what appeared to be fragments of Arabic writing. These, presumably, were the "real" documents. I asked to examine the Arabic originals, but to date the committee has not provided them. In a recent letter to me they say that the originals are actually in Baghdad and that I will have to apply to the puppet government if I want to have them examined forensically. So much for the integrity of the documents. And for Coleman's case.

After the invasion, a massive forgery industry sprang up in Iraq. I had already been a victim of it and had subsequently won substantial libel damages, as discussed earlier, from the *Christian Science Monitor,* which ran a series of the forged documents accusing me of much the same thing that I was peremptorily convicted of by Coleman's committee. The *Mail on Sunday* had bought another batch. All of these had been proved to be fakes, and as any amateur sleuth could have discovered, I hadn't even been in the country when several meetings where cash was handed over were supposed to have taken place.

In the shadowy background to all this was Ahmed Chalabi, whose machinations had been crucial in moving President George W. Bush to war. Chalabi had been in charge of the Iraqi oil ministry after the fall of the Saddam regime. Subsequently he was raided by U.S. forces and accused of corruption, but he is now effectively back in charge of the oil industry and is one of the top Iraqi ministers running the country. The strong suspicion was that Chalabi had a hand in the "finding" of these documents.

The case against me rested on these "translated" oil documents on which appeared either my name, that of the Mariam Appeal, or that of Fawaz Zureikat, chairman of the defunct campaign. In addition, unnamed officials, together with the former vice-president of Iraq, Taha Yasin Ramadan, now in U.S. custody in Abu Ghraib prison and facing a probable death sentence, had been interviewed by the committee and were said to have testified that I received the allocations. These were the same people, as I pointed out, who had been accused of being liars, cheats and genocidal maniacs before the invasion.

In the run-up to my appearance our press statements had likened the Coleman committee to that of Senator Joe McCarthy, the rabid anti-communist, who put some of the most famous names in Hollywood through his show trials. I was determined to emphasize this comparison in my introductory remarks so I opened with a play on perhaps the most famous phrase ever heard at the House Un-American Activities Committee:

"Senator, I am not now, nor have I ever been, an oil trader and neither has anyone on my behalf. I have never seen a barrel of oil, owned one, bought one, sold one—and neither has anyone on my behalf."

After the first couple of sentences, judging by the gasps and occasional embarrassed titters I could hear coming from the audience behind me, I already knew that we were going to be able to refute all of the committee's allegations. But I didn't let up, delivering what I hoped was a sequence of fatal blows. My testimony was going out around the world, on Sky television to the UK and Europe, on C-Span in the United States, live on radio from London to Lebanon, on al-Jazeera to the Arab world. It would later be edited and played as the news lead of the day on several continents.

The questioning by the two Senators that followed my opening statement was desultory. Carl Levin, the Democrat, tried to pin me down about sanctions-busting. If Zureikat had paid kickbacks to the Iraq government, he asked, would I find that reprehensible? I was not going to be trapped into making a statement that implicated my friend or accepted in any way the rectitude of the sanctions legislation. I made clear that I had always opposed the UN sanctions laws, that they were responsible for the deaths of tens of thousands in Iraq, that the income they provided for each Iraqi citizen was just 30 cents a day.

There was a slightly bizarre and unsettling postscript to the questions over Zureikat. When we returned to Britain, Ron received information that our friend the businessman was again involved in trading with Iraq, supplying scrambler chips for mobile phones and communications devices, paid for in U.S. dollars by the American-controlled administration in Baghdad. So the man who stood accused alongside me at the Senate inquiry, who had allegedly flouted the sanctions law by providing bribes to the Saddam regime and who was being sought by the UN investigators, was again trading with Iraq, but now with the clear agreement of the U.S. government.

When Ron called Fawaz he denied the Senate allegations that he had acted illegally, adding that he had been interviewed by US government agencies and that his "punishment" for his previous oil dealings was an agreement that he could do business with the new, American-backed regime. Coleman's committee was clearly unaware that the alleged sanctions-breaker, on whose back the whole case against me rested, was now officially approved by the U.S. government.

As noon neared the two Senators ran out of questions. In the boxing ring there comes a point when you see the light die in the eyes of your adversary. It is a moment when one knows that one's opponent no longer wishes to be there, knows that he cannot prevail. Thus it was with Senator Coleman. I heard Ron whisper in my ear "he's really struggling now." In the absence of a bell to save him, Coleman threw in the towel. Not since Marciano flattened the horizontal chump Don Cockell had there been a massacre like it. But this time, the British guy won.

The whole case against me which, until then, I hadn't had the opportunity to contest, was based on documents that weren't original and that could not be tested, and witnesses being held under the torture regime at Abu Ghraib and other prisons whose statements I did not see and who I could not question. Any reasonable person might think that such evidence would be inadmissible but here it formed the centerpiece of the prosecution.

It had all passed by in a blaze. The highly adversarial British parliamentary system had had its day out against its much more decorous and unchallenging American counterpart and had come out on top. Coleman would later state that the hearing had not been a contest but most of the media, even including administration supporters, seemed to agree that I had won. I knew I had done pretty well, although I did not appreciate the resonance of my words for a huge number of people around the world. I can only say that God gave me wings that day.

After the hearing another media scrum convened in the corridor. Eventually, when a Senate attendant intervened and curtailed it, we all spilled onto the sidewalk outside. I was dragged around the corner to a dais located in some nearby parkland where I gave a series of one-on-one interviews with more media than I can possibly recall. Eventually I took off the lapel mic—but not before responding to a question from CNN about whether I was, indeed, a wealthy man. "One of your guys has just told me the sole of my shoe is hanging off," I replied. I lifted the shoe towards the camera. "And I'm staying in probably the worst hotel in Washington. It's so bad even the cockroaches have deserted it." The last two sentences were cut from the broadcast.

I had traveled 3,000 miles for a Senate appearance that lasted just 47 minutes. Now it was over. The three of us then walked off through the park toward Union Station and a cup of coffee "I think I did all right there," I said hopefully to my companions. No one disagreed.

I finished off a few more interviews and then, with the sun still high in the sky, jumped into a taxi for the airport. There was a Respect rally back in London to speak at the following evening. I slumped into the airline seat and in minutes I was asleep, not waking until I was shaken by the cabin attendant as the plane neared Heathrow.

TESTIMONY BEFORE THE
U.S. SENATE

Committee on Homeland Security and Governmental Affairs

SUBCOMMITTEE ON INVESTIGATIONS (MAY 17, 2005)

SEN. COLEMAN: Mr. Galloway, I'm pleased to have you before the committee today.

What I'm going to do is briefly summarize the evidence before we give you a chance to give your sworn testimony.

The Oil-for-Food program was used to support those who were favorable to Iraq. Former Iraqi Deputy Prime Minister Tariq Aziz and Iraqi Vice President Taha Yassin Ramadan confirmed this.

I would think that you would admit that your efforts to oppose the sanction were well received by the regime. I know it's been quoted to you many, many times—but your, I would say, infamous statement to Saddam Hussein on January 21, 1994, where you said to Saddam, "Your Excellency, Mr. President, I greet you in the name of many thousands of people in Britain who stood against the tide and opposed the war of aggression against Iraq and continue to oppose the war by economic means, which is aimed to strangle the life out of the great people of Iraq."

You then went on to say you greet the Palestinian people, you went on to note that you thought "the president would appreciate knowing that even today three years after the war I still meet with families who are calling their newborn 'son of Saddam.'"

You went on ultimately at the very end to say, "Sir, I salute your strength, your courage, your indefatigability, and I want you to know that we are with you." And I believe it was in Arabic 'thowra hat'l nas'r, thowra hat'l nasr, thowra hat'l quds', which means "Until victory, until victory, until victory in Jerusalem." And I also would note that you would say that you deeply regret those comments and that the comments were not aimed directly at Saddam but were aimed at the Iraqi people.

In the fall of 1999 you headed a two-month

London-to-Baghdad bus trip to gain support for lifting the sanctions on Iraq.

We have your name on Iraqi documents, some prepared before the fall of Saddam, some after that, which identify you as one of the allocation holders, that your allocations were then used by Fawaz Zureikat, operating under the name of Aredio Petroleum and Middle East Advanced Semiconductor to actually lift the oil.

We note too, based on the statements of former Iraqi officials as well as some documents and in the cases of Vladimir Zhirinovsky and Alexander Voloshin correspondence in documents, that allocation holders knew that surcharges or oil allocations were paid to Saddam Hussein, and that allocation holders were aware of this and were responsible for the payments.

We have also heard testimony regarding several documents retrieved from the Iraqi Ministry of Oil that demonstrate how Iraq allocated oil to its friends and allies.

That chart also lists Contract N1104 with Middle East Advanced Semiconductor.

Footnote 93. Your testimony regarding a SOMO commercial invoice dated June 27, 2002, that shows Middle East Semiconductor loaded 2,360,860 barrels of Iraqi crude oil pursuant to SOMO crude oil sales contract N1104.

Exhibit 12. We heard testimony regarding correspondence between the executive director of SOMO to the Iraqi Oil Minister providing details of contract N1104 and listing your name in parentheses, next to Middle East Advanced Semiconductor and Fawaz Zureikat, who we know lifted the oil. Again statements of detainees, including former Vice President Ramadan, confirm that the name in parentheses—your name—is the allocation holder.

Your testimony regarding Contract N1104, which was signed on December 12, 2001, between SOMO and Fawaz Zureikat, president of Middle East Advanced Semiconductor.

Your testimony regarding SOMO commercial invoice B13201 that shows Aredio Petroleum lifted 1,014,403 barrels of Iraqi oil pursuant to SOMO crude oil sales contract N923.

Exhibit 45. We heard testimony regarding SOMO chart entitled "Crude Oil Allocation during Phase 9 Memorandum of Understanding" that indicates that contract N923 was executed between

SOMO and Mr. Fawaz Zureikat (slash) George Galloway (slash) Aredio Petroleum.

Exhibit 9. We also heard testimony regarding the memo from the executive director of SOMO to the Oil Minister requesting approval of contract N923. The document includes an official Ministry of Oil stamp dated 1/15/2001 and provides details of a contract N923 signed with Aredio Petroleum Company, (parens) Fawaz Zureikat (dash) Mariam's Appeal, indicating that the allocation recipient of the contract N923 was Fawaz Zureikat—Mariam's Appeal.

Mr. Galloway, as I indicated in my opening statement, this is not a court of law. This committee has simply made available information obtained during the investigation from interviews with former Iraqi officials and Iraqi documents to lay out how the Oil-for-Food program worked—how allocations were given to favored friends, how allocation holders made substantial commissions on those allocations to oil companies, what Ramadan called "compensation for support."

But another official in talking about another allocation holder said, "Of course they made a profit.

That's the whole point." Surcharges and oil contracts were given back to the Saddam regime and were the responsibility of the allocation holder.

The evidence clearly indicates you as an allocation beneficiary, who transferred the allocations to Fawaz Zureikat, who became chairman of your organization Mariam's Appeal.

Senior Iraqi officials have confirmed that you in fact received oil allocations and that the documents that identify you as an allocation recipient are valid.

If you can help provide any evidence that challenges the veracity of these documents or the statements of former Iraqi officials, we'd welcome that input.

Mr. Galloway, you're appearing before the subcommittee without asserting any privilege or immunity. Indeed, your appearance before the subcommittee is entirely voluntary and on your own accord. No subpoena was issued to secure your appearance.

You're appearing before the subcommittee concerning matters that do not arise out of the performance of any of your official duties as a member of the British Parliament but instead concern actions taken by you in your capacity as a private citizen.

Before we begin, pursuant to Rule 6, all witnesses who testify before this subcommittee are required to be sworn.

At this time I'd ask you to rise and please raise your right hand.

[Swearing in]

We'll be using a timing system today, Mr. Galloway. You have ten minutes for an opening statement. If you need more time, we'll certainly accommodate that, and you may proceed.

GALLOWAY: Senator, I am not now, nor have I ever been, an oil trader. And neither has anyone on my behalf. I have never seen a barrel of oil, owned one, bought one, sold one—and neither has anyone on my behalf.

Now I know that standards have slipped in the last few years in Washington, but for a lawyer you are remarkably cavalier with any idea of justice. I am here today but last week you already found me guilty. You traduced my name around the world without ever having asked me a single question, without ever having contacted me, without ever having written to me or telephoned me, without any attempt to contact me whatsoever. And you call that justice.

Now I want to deal with the pages that relate to me in this dossier and I want to point out areas where there are—let's be charitable and say errors. Then I want to put this in the context where I believe it ought to be. On the very first page of your document about me you assert that I have had "many meetings" with Saddam Hussein. This is false.

I have had two meetings with Saddam Hussein, once in 1994 and once in August of 2002. By no stretch of the English language can that be described as many meetings with Saddam Hussein.

As a matter of fact, I have met Saddam Hussein exactly the same number of times as Donald Rumsfeld met him. The difference is Donald Rumsfeld met him to sell him guns and to give him maps the better to target those guns. I met him to try and bring about an end to sanctions, suffering and war, and on the second of the two occasions, I met him to try and persuade him to let Dr. Hans Blix and the United Nations weapons inspectors back into the country—a rather better use of two meetings with

Saddam Hussein than your own Secretary of State for Defense made of his.

I was an opponent of Saddam Hussein when British and Americans governments and business-men were selling him guns and gas. I used to demonstrate outside the Iraqi embassy when British and American officials were going in and doing commerce.

You will see from the official parliamentary record, Hansard, from the 15th March 1990 on-wards, voluminous evidence that I have a rather bet-ter record of opposition to Saddam Hussein than you do and than any other member of the British or American governments do.

Now you say in this document, you quote a source, you have the gall to quote a source, without ever having asked me whether the allegation from the source is true, that I am "the owner of a company which has made substantial profits from trading in Iraqi oil."

Senator, I do not own any companies, beyond a small company whose entire purpose, whose sole purpose, is to receive the income from my journalis-tic earnings from my employer, Associated Newspapers, in London. I do not own a company that's been trading in Iraqi oil. And you have no business to carry a quotation, utterly unsubstantiated and false, implying otherwise.

Now you have nothing on me, Senator, except my name on lists of names from Iraq, many of which have been drawn up after the installation of your puppet government in Baghdad. If you had any of the letters against me that you had against Zhirinovsky, and even Pasqua, they would have been up there in your slideshow for the members of your committee today.

You have my name on lists provided to you by the Duelfer inquiry, provided to him by the convicted bank robber, and fraudster, and conman Ahmed Chalabi, who many people in your country to their credit now realize played a decisive role in leading your country into the disaster in Iraq.

There were 270 names on that list originally. That's somehow been filleted down to the names you chose to deal with in this committee. Some of the names on that committee included the former secretary to his Holiness Pope John Paul II, the former head of the African National Congress Presidential office and many others who had one defining characteristic in common: they all stood against the policy of sanctions and war which you vociferously prosecuted and which has led us to this disaster.

You quote Mr. Dahar Yassein Ramadan. Well, you have something on me, I've never met Mr. Dahar Yassein Ramadan. Your sub-committee apparently has. But I do know that he's your prisoner, I believe he's in Abu Ghraib prison. I believe he is facing war crimes charges, punishable by death. In these circumstances, knowing what the world knows about how you treat prisoners in Abu Ghraib prison, in Bagram Airbase, in Guantánamo Bay, including I may say, British citizens being held in those places, I'm not sure how much credibility anyone would put on anything you manage to get from a prisoner in those circumstances. But you quote 13 words from Dahar Yassein Ramadan, whom I have never met. If he said what he said, then he is wrong.

And if you had any evidence that I had ever engaged in any actual oil transaction, if you had any evidence that anybody ever gave me any money, it would be before the public and before this committee today because I agreed with your Mr. Greenblatt [Mark Greenblatt, legal counsel on the committee].

Your Mr. Greenblatt was absolutely correct.

What counts is not the names on the paper, what counts is where's the money. Senator? Who paid me hundreds of thousands of dollars of money? The answer to that is nobody. And if you had anybody who ever paid me a penny, you would have produced them today.

Now you refer at length to a company named in these documents as Aredio Petroleum. I say to you under oath here today: I have never heard of this company, I have never met anyone from this company. This company has never paid a penny to me and I'll tell you something else: I can assure you that Aredio Petroleum has never paid a single penny to the Mariam Appeal Campaign. Not a thin dime. I don't know who Aredio Petroleum are, but I daresay if you were to ask them they would confirm that they have never met me or ever paid me a penny.

Whilst I'm on that subject, who is this senior former regime official that you spoke to yesterday? Don't you think I have a right to know? Don't you think the Committee and the public have a right to know who this senior former regime official you were quoting against me interviewed yesterday actually is?

Now, one of the most serious of the mistakes

you have made in this set of documents is, to be frank, such a schoolboy howler as to make a fool of the efforts that you have made. You assert on page 19, not once but twice, that the documents that you are referring to cover a different period in time from the documents covered by the *Daily Telegraph* which were a subject of a libel action won by me in the High Court in England late last year.

You state that The *Daily Telegraph* article cited documents from 1992 and 1993 whilst you are dealing with documents dating from 2001. Senator, the *Daily Telegraph's* documents date identically to the documents that you were dealing with in your report here. None of the *Daily Telegraph's* documents dealt with a period of 1992, 1993. I had never set foot in Iraq until late in 1993—never in my life. There could possibly be no documents relating to Oil-for-Food matters in 1992, 1993, for the Oil-for-Food scheme did not exist at that time.

And yet you've allocated a full section of this document to claiming that your documents are from a different era to the *Daily Telegraph* documents when the opposite is true. Your documents and the *Daily Telegraph* documents deal with exactly the same period.

But perhaps you were confusing the *Daily Telegraph* action with the *Christian Science Monitor*. The *Christian Science Monitor* did indeed publish on its front pages a set of allegations against me very similar to the ones that your committee have made. They did indeed rely on documents which started in 1992, 1993. These documents were unmasked by the *Christian Science Monitor* themselves as forgeries.

Now, the neo-con websites and newspapers in which you're such a hero, senator, were all absolutely cock-a-hoop at the publication of the *Christian Science Monitor* documents, they were all absolutely convinced of their authenticity. They were all absolutely convinced that these documents showed me receiving $10 million from the Saddam regime. And they were all lies.

In the same week as the *Daily Telegraph* published their documents against me, the *Christian Science Monitor* published theirs which turned out to be forgeries and the British newspaper, *Mail on Sunday,* purchased a third set of documents which also upon forensic examination turned out to be forgeries. So there's nothing fanciful about this. Nothing at all fanciful about it.

The existence of forged documents implicating me in commercial activities with the Iraqi regime is a proven fact. It's a proven fact that these forged documents existed and were being circulated amongst right-wing newspapers in Baghdad and around the world in the immediate aftermath of the fall of the Iraqi regime.

Now, Senator, I gave my heart and soul to oppose the policy that you promoted. I gave my political life's blood to try to stop the mass killing of Iraqis by the sanctions on Iraq which killed one million Iraqis, most of them children, most of them died before they even knew that they were Iraqis, but they died for no other reason other than that they were Iraqis with the misfortune to born at that time. I gave my heart and soul to stop you committing the disaster that you did commit in invading Iraq. And I told the world that your case for the war was a pack of lies.

I told the world that Iraq, contrary to your claims, did not have weapons of mass destruction. I told the world, contrary to your claims, that Iraq had no connection to al-Qaeda. I told the world, contrary to your claims, that Iraq had no connection to the atrocity on 9/11, 2001. I told the world, contrary to your claims, that the Iraqi people would resist a British and American invasion of their country and that the fall of Baghdad would not be the beginning of the end, but merely the end of the beginning.

Senator, in everything I said about Iraq, I turned out to be right and you turned out to be wrong and 100,000 people paid with their lives; 1600 of them American soldiers sent to their deaths on a pack of lies; 15,000 of them wounded, many of them disabled forever on a pack of lies.

If the world had listened to Kofi Annan, whose dismissal you demanded, if the world had listened to President Chirac who you want to paint as some kind of corrupt traitor, if the world had listened to me and the anti-war movement in Britain, we would not be in the disaster that we are in today. Senator, this is the mother of all smokescreens. You are trying to divert attention from the crimes that you supported, from the theft of billions of dollars of Iraq's wealth.

Have a look at the real Oil-for-Food scandal. Have a look at the 14 months you were in charge of Baghdad, the first 14 months when $8.8 billion of Iraq's wealth went missing on your watch. Have a look at Halliburton and other American corporations that stole not only Iraq's money, but the money of the American taxpayer.

Have a look at the oil that you didn't even meter, that you were shipping out of the country and selling, the proceeds of which went who knows where? Have a look at the $800 million you gave to American military commanders to hand out around the country without even counting it or weighing it.

Have a look at the real scandal breaking in the newspapers today, revealed in the earlier testimony in this committee. That the biggest sanctions busters were not me or Russian politicians or French politicians. The real sanctions busters were your own companies with the connivance of your own government.

SEN. COLEMAN: Thank you, Mr. Galloway.

Mr. Galloway, can we start by talking about Fawaz Zureikat. Do you know the individual?

GALLOWAY: I know him very well.

SEN. COLEMAN: In fact you were best man at his wedding?

GALLOWAY: I was.

SEN. COLEMAN: And at some point in time he became chair of Mariam's Appeals. Is that correct?

GALLOWAY: He did. Yeah.

SEN. COLEMAN: And can you tell me when that occurred?

GALLOWAY: I think in late 2000 or early 2001.

SEN. COLEMAN: Before Mr. Zureikat was chair of Mariam's Appeal, who had that position?

GALLOWAY: I was the founding chairman.

SEN. COLEMAN: Was there someone between you and—

GALLOWAY: Mr. Halford.

SEN. COLEMAN: And do you recall when he had that position?

GALLOWAY: I don't.

SEN. COLEMAN: Mr. Zureikat was a significant contributor to Mariam's Appeals. Is that correct?

GALLOWAY: He was the second biggest contributor. The main contributor was Sheik Zayed, the ruler of the United Arab Emirates, which you've glossed over in your report because it's slightly embarrassing to you. And the third major contributor was the Crown Prince of Saudi Arabia, which you've equally glossed over because it's embarrassing to you.

And both of those individuals are your friends.

SEN. COLEMAN: How much did Mr. Zureikat contribute to Mariam's Appeals?

GALLOWAY: Roughly 375,000 English pounds.

SEN. COLEMAN: About $600,000?

GALLOWAY: I don't know the conversion. But it's 375,000 Sterling.

SEN. COLEMAN: If you can, uh . . . By the way, Mr. Zureikat was your representative—uh, designated representative—for the activities of Mariam's Appeals. Is that correct?

GALLOWAY: For the activities of Mariam's Appeals. Yes.

SEN. COLEMAN: And when did he get that position?

GALLOWAY: I think late 2000.

SEN. COLEMAN: Late 2000. Looking at Exhibit 9—and I think you have the books in front of you—that appears to be a document from the Ministry of Oil that testimony has indicated that the signature is an accurate signature.

Do you have any reason to believe that that document is false?

GALLOWAY: Well, I have told you that I have never heard of Aredio Petroleum, and I've told you that the Mariam Appeal never received a single penny from Aredio Petroleum. So the information at the top of the page, if you've translated it accurately, is false.

SEN. COLEMAN: Have you heard of Middle East ASI company?

GALLOWAY: Yes. That's Mr. Zureikat's company.

SEN. COLEMAN: I turn to Exhibit 12.

And that purports again to be a stamp of the Ministry of Oil of Iraq and this purports to be showing the details of a contract signed with Middle East ASI company, Mr. George Galloway and Fuwaz Zureikat. So Middle East ASI is Mr. Zureikat's company?

GALLOWAY: Middle East ASI is Mr. Zureikat's company. He may well have signed an oil contract. It had nothing to do with me.

SEN. COLEMAN: He was chair of Mariam's

Appeals in 2000. I take it you knew him well. Did he ever talk with you about his dealings with oil in Iraq?

GALLOWAY: He did better than that. He talked to everybody. He talked to every English journalist that came through Baghdad—who he helped at our request to get the interviews and to get to the places that they wanted and needed to go. He was introduced to everyone as a major benefactor of the Mariam Appeal and as a businessman doing extensive business in Iraq and elsewhere in the Middle East.

SEN. COLEMAN: I'm asking you specifically, in 2001 were you aware he was doing oil deals with Iraq?

GALLOWAY: I was aware that he was doing extensive business with Iraq. I did not know the details of it. It was not my business.

SEN. COLEMAN: So this is somebody who was the chairman of committee that you know well and you're not able to say that he was . . .

GALLOWAY: Well, there's a lot of contributors—I've just been checking—to your political campaigns.

SEN. COLEMAN: There's not many at that level, Mr. Galloway—

GALLOWAY: I've checked your website. There are lots of contributors to your political campaign funds. I don't suppose you ask any of them how they made the money they give you.

SEN. COLEMAN: Certainly not at $600,000 American.

But let me ask you again, just so that the record is clear—that it's clear on the record—that you're not contesting then the validity of Document 12, Exhibit 12. You're indicating that Mr. Zureikat could have had dealings with Iraq. You're saying that at that point in time you're not aware that he had oil dealings with Iraq?

GALLOWAY: First of all, I've only seen this document today. And I'm telling you that insofar as my name is in a parenthesis the information in it is false.

I've no reason to believe that Mr. Zureikat's company didn't do that particular oil deal.

But this is your problem in this whole affair. There is nobody arguing that Mr. Zureikat's company did not do oil transactions and many other—much bigger, frankly—business contracts with Iraq. There is nobody contesting that Mr. Zureikat made substantial donations to our campaign against sanctions and war.

My point is—you have accused me, personally, of enriching myself, of taking money from Iraq. And that is false and unjust.

SEN. COLEMAN: Mr. Galloway, do you recall an interview you had with a Jeremy Paxman in April 23 of 2003,

[Addressing aide] Can we have a copy of the transcript of that?

I'd like to refresh your memory.

[To aide] Can you get a copy of that.

As we get you a copy, you were asked a question, talking about business dealings with Mr. Zureikat in

Iraq. And at the least the transcript that I have—and I'd ask you to let me know if it's incorrect—your quote is, something about business in Iraq

"Well, I'm trying to reach him"—this is in 2003—"I'm trying to reach him to ask him if he's ever been involved in oil deals because I don't know the answer to that." So in 2003 you're saying you don't know the answer to whether he was involved in oil deals?

GALLOWAY: Well, I told you in my previous two answers—I knew that Mr. Zureikat was heavily involved in business in Iraq and elsewhere, but that it was none of my business what particular transactions or business he was involved in—any more than you ask the American and Israel Public Affairs Committee [AIPAC] when they donate money to you or pay for your trips to Israel, where they got the money from.

SEN. COLEMAN: So Mr. Galloway, you would have this committee believe that your designated representative from the Mariam's Appeal becomes the chair of the Mariam's Appeal, was listed in Iraqi documents as obviously doing business, oil deals with Iraq, that you never had a conversation with him in 2001 on whether he was doing oil business with Iraq.

GALLOWAY: No, I'm doing better than that. I'm telling you that I knew that he was doing a vast amount of business with Iraq. Much bigger, as I said a couple of answers ago, than any oil business he did. In the airports he was the representative of some of the world's biggest companies in Iraq. He was an extremely wealthy businessman doing very extensive business in Iraq.

Not only did I know that, but I told everyone about it. I emblazoned it in our literature, on our website, precisely so that people like you could not later credibly question my bonafides in that regard. So I did better than that.

I never asked him if he was trading in oil. I knew he was a big trader with Iraq, and I told everybody about it.

SEN. COLEMAN: So in 2003, when you said you didn't know whether he was doing oil deals, were you telling the truth at that time?

GALLOWAY: Yes, I was. I've never known until the *Telegraph* story appeared that he was alleged to be doing oil deals. But his oil deals are about one-tenth of the business that he did in Iraq. So I did better than telling people about his oil deals. I told them he was doing much, much more than that.

SEN. COLEMAN: So Exhibit 14, which purports to be a contract with Middle East Semiconductor, Contract M1214. Middle East Semiconductor, again, is Mr. Zureikat's company, is that correct?

GALLOWAY: Yes, it is.

SEN. COLEMAN: So do you have any reason to believe that this document is false?

GALLOWAY: Well, the parenthesis, if the parenthesis implies—as you've been arguing all morning that it implies—that this was being signed for by Middle East Advanced Semiconductors in order to pass the money on to me, is false.

Mr. Zureikat and Middle East Semiconductors or any other company have never given me any money. And if they had, you would have it up here on a board, and in front of the committee here.

SEN. COLEMAN: I take it, Mr. Galloway, that in regard to any surcharges paid to Saddam—I think it's Footnote 89, which refers to the surcharge for the contract, focused on Mariam's Appeal—you're saying that that document, first of all, any contract between Iraq and Mariam's Appeals is false?

GALLOWAY: Well, Senator, I had gotten used to the allegation that I was taking money from Saddam Hussein. It's actually surreal to hear in this room this morning that I'm being accused of giving money *to* Saddam Hussein.

This is utterly preposterous, utterly preposterous, that I gave $300,000 to Saddam Hussein. This is beyond the realms of the ridiculous.

Now. The Mariam Appeals finances have been investigated by the Charity Commission on the order of Lord Goldsmith.

(You'll recall him, Senator. He's the attorney general. Practically the only lawman in the world that thought your war with Iraq was legal, thought Britain joining your war with Iraq was legal.)

He ordered the Charity Commission to investigate the Mariam Appeal. Using their statutory powers, they recovered all money in and all money out ever received or spent by the Mariam Appeal. They found no impropriety. And I can assure you, they found no money from an oil contract from Aredio Petroleum—none whatsoever.

SEN. COLEMAN: And the commission did not look at these documents relating to this contract with Iraq. Is that correct?—

GALLOWAY: —No, but they looked better than that, Senator.—

SEN. COLEMAN: —I'm not asking you better. I'm asking the question whether they looked at these documents.—

GALLOWAY: —Senator, you're not listening to what I am saying. They did better than that.

They looked at every penny in and every penny

out. And they did not find, I can assure you, any trace of a donation from a company called Aredio Petroleum, or, frankly, a donation from any company other than Mr. Zureikat's company. That's a fact.

SEN. COLEMAN: If I can get back to Mr. Zureikat one more time. Do you recall a time when he specifically—when you had a conversation with him about oil dealings in Iraq?

GALLOWAY: I have already answered that question. I can assure you, Mr. Zureikat never gave me a penny from an oil deal, from a cake deal, from a bread deal, or from any deal. He donated money to our campaign, which we publicly brandished on all of our literature, along with the other donors to the campaign.

SEN. COLEMAN: Again, Mr. Galloway, a simple question. I'm looking for either a yes or no. Did you ever have a conversation with Mr. Zureikat where he informed you that he had oil dealings with Iraq, yes or no?

GALLOWAY: Not before this *Daily Telegraph* report, no.

SEN. COLEMAN: Senator Levin.

SEN. CARL LEVIN (D): Thank you, Mr. Galloway.

Mr. Galloway, could you take a look at the Exhibit Number 12 . . .

GALLOWAY: Yes.

SEN. LEVIN: . . . where your name is in parenthesis after Mr. Zureikat's?—

GALLOWAY: Before Mr. Zureikat's, if I'm looking at the right exhibit—

SEN. LEVIN: I'm sorry. I was going to finish my sentence—my question, though. My question was, where your name is in parenthesis after Mr. Zureikat's company.

GALLOWAY: I apologize, Senator.

SEN. LEVIN: That's all right. Now, that document—assuming it's an accurate translation of the document underneath it—would you . . . you're not alleging here today that the document is a forgery, I gather?

GALLOWAY: Well, I have no idea, Senator, if it's a forgery or not.

SEN. LEVIN: But you're not alleging.

GALLOWAY: I'm saying that the information insofar as it relates to me is fake.

SEN. LEVIN: I—is wrong?

GALLOWAY: It's wrong.

SEN. LEVIN: But you're not alleging that the document—

GALLOWAY: Well, I have no way of knowing, Senator.

SEN. LEVIN: That's fine. So you're not alleging?

GALLOWAY: No, I have no way—I have no way of knowing. This is the first time—

SEN. LEVIN: Is it fair to say since you don't know, you're not alleging?

GALLOWAY: Well, it would have been nice to have seen it before today.

SEN. LEVIN: Is it fair to say, though, that either because you've not seen it before or because—otherwise, you don't know. You're not alleging the document's a fake. Is that fair to say?

GALLOWAY: I haven't had it in my possession long enough to form a view about that.

SEN. LEVIN: All right. Would you let the subcommittee know after you've had it in your possession long enough whether you consider the document a fake.

GALLOWAY: Yes, although there is a—there is an academic quality about it, Senator Levin, because you have already found me guilty before you—

before you actually allowed me to come here and speak for myself.

SEN. LEVIN: Well, in order to attempt to clear your name, would you . . .

GALLOWAY: Well, let's be clear about something.

SEN. LEVIN: Well, let me finish my question. Let me be clear about that, first of all.

Would you submit to the subcommittee after you've had a chance to review this document whether or not, in your judgment, it is a forgery? Will you do that?

GALLOWAY: Well, if you will give me the original. I mean, this is not—presumably, you wrote this English translation.

SEN. LEVIN: Yes, and there's a copy underneath it of the—

GALLOWAY: Well, yes, there is a copy of a

gray blur. If you'll give me—if you'll give me the original—

SEN. LEVIN: The copy of the original.

[Crosstalk]

GALLOWAY: Give me the original in a decipherable way, then of course I'll—

SEN. LEVIN: That would be fine. We appreciate that. .

GALLOWAY: Yes.

SEN. LEVIN: Now, at the bottom of this document, assuming—assuming it's not a forgery for a moment, it says "surcharge." Are we together?

GALLOWAY: Yes.

SEN. LEVIN: "As per the instructions of Your Excellency over the phone on 12/11/01 of not accepting the company's proposal unless they pay the debt incurred since phase eight."

If, in fact—if, in fact, Mr. Zureikat's company paid a surcharge or a kickback to the Iraqi government in order to obtain an allocation of oil, would that trouble you?

GALLOWAY: Well, as it turns out, from your own testimony, that practically everyone in the world, and especially the United States, was paying kickbacks.

SEN. LEVIN: My question. . . . It troubles me a great deal. As you've heard from my statement today, I'm very much troubled that we have an oil company that was involved in this and we're going to go after that oil company.

Now let me ask you. I've expressed my view about Bayoil. So now let met ask you about Mr. Zureikat's company.

If in fact Mr. Zureikat's company paid a kickback to the Iraqi government in order to obtain this allocation, would you be troubled? That's my question.

GALLOWAY: Yeah. That's a good question. And will you allow me to answer it seriously and not in a yes-or-no fashion? Because I could give you a glib—

SEN. LEVIN: Providing you give us an answer, I'd be delighted to hear it.

GALLOWAY: Here's my answer and I hope it does delight you.

I opposed the Oil-for-Food program with all my heart. Not for the reasons that you are troubled by, but because it was a program which saw the death—I'm talking about the death now; I'm talking about a mass grave—of a million people, most of them children, in Iraq. The Oil-for-Food program gave 30 cents per day per Iraqi for the period of the Oil-for-Food program—30 cents for all food, all medicine, all clothes, all schools, all hospitals, all public services. I believe that the United Nations had no right to starve Iraq's people because it had fallen out with Iraq's dictator.

David Bonior, your former colleague, Senator, whom I admired very much—a former chief whip here on the Hill—described the sanctions policy as "infanticide masquerading as politics." Senator Coleman thinks that's funny, but I think it's the most profound description of that era that I have ever read—infanticide masquerading as politics.

So I opposed this program with all my heart. Not because Saddam was getting kickbacks from it—and I don't know when it's alleged these kickbacks started. Not because some individuals were getting rich doing business with Iraq under it. But because it was a murderous policy of killing huge numbers of Iraqis. That's what troubles *me*. That's what troubles me.

Now, if you're asking me, "Is Mr. Zureikat in some difficulty?"—like all the other companies that it would appear paid kickbacks to the Iraqi regime—no doubt he is. Although it would appear he's quite small beer compared to the American companies that were involved in the same thing.

SEN. LEVIN: Now my question . . .

GALLOWAY: That's what—I told you what troubles me.

SEN. LEVIN: I'm not asking you—[Crosstalk]
My question . . . Now that you've given us your statement about your feeling about the Oil-for-

Food program—My question is, Would you be troubled if you knew that Mr. Zureikat paid a kickback in order to get an allocation of an oil contract? That's a very simple question.

GALLOWAY: It's Mr. Zureikat's problem, not mine.

SEN. LEVIN: It would not trouble you?

GALLOWAY: It's Mr. Zureikat's problem, not mine.

SEN. LEVIN: And so that if a kickback, which was illegal under international—now you may not agree with the U.N., but that's the international community that you're attacking, which is fine. You're entitled to do that. You're entitled and I'll defend your right to do it. But you're attacking a U.N. program—which is your right to do—which was aimed at providing humanitarian assistance to try to alleviate the problems that the sanctions provided—which is your right to do. But my question—which you are so far evading—is, Would you be troubled if that U.N. Oil-for-Food program was being circum-vented by the kind of kickbacks which were taking place and being given to Saddam Hussein in order to obtain allocations under that program *if* Mr. Zureikat participated in that kickback scheme, which violated the U.N. sanc . . . You may not have agreed with it, but it violated the program. Would it trouble you if he violated that U.N. program in that way? That's my question.

GALLOWAY: Senator, there are many things—

SEN. LEVIN: I know. Other things trouble you. But can you just give us a straightforward answer? You've given us a long explanation of other things that trouble you, which is your right. Now I'm asking you whether *that* troubles you.

GALLOWAY: It troubles me that it might put him in difficulty. It troubles me that it might now lead to a prosecution of him. It troubles me that this will be further smoke in the smokescreen. But I, root and branch, opposed this [SEN. LEVIN: I understand . . .] Oil-for-Food program.

SEN. LEVIN: There were a lot of things you

opposed, but you don't believe should be circum-vented in illegal ways. Isn't that—

GALLOWAY: But, please, Senator! You sup-ported the illegal attack on Iraq. Don't talk to me about illegality—

SEN. LEVIN: Sorry about that. I didn't. But that's beside the point. [Crosstalk] That's beside the point. You're wrong in your—

GALLOWAY: Well, I'm collectively talking about the Senate. Not you personally.

SEN. LEVIN: Well, that's okay. Let me go back to my question. I don't want to get involved in—

GALLOWAY: Why not? You want to talk about illegality?

SEN. LEVIN: No.

GALLOWAY: You launched an illegal war, which has killed 100,000 people. You want me to be troubled?

SEN. LEVIN: No, I want you to answer questions which are fairly put and directly in front of you. Now I'll ask you one last—two last questions. *If*—if—Mr. Zureikat's contribution to Mariam's Appeal came from the sale of oil—or his share of the sale from oil—which he was able to obtain because he paid a kickback in violation of the U.N. program. Would that contribution trouble you? That's my question.

GALLOWAY: Well, Senator—

SEN. LEVIN: If you can't give a short answer, just—

GALLOWAY: I'll give as short as I can, and I appreciate your fairness in this.

Fundraising for political purposes is seldom pretty, as any American politician could testify. I took the view—I can be criticized for it, have been criticized for it—that I would fundraise from the kings of Arabia whose political systems I have opposed all my life in order to raise funds for what I thought was an emergency, facing a disaster. And I did not ask Mr. Zureikat which part of his profits

from his entire business empire he was making donations to our—

SEN. LEVIN: That wasn't my question. My
question was, would it trouble you if you found
that out?

It's okay. You're not going to answer. I want to go
to my next question.

You're simply not going to answer. I will say,
American politicians who find the source of money
after it's given to them is troubling—they find out
something they didn't know afterwards—frequently
will—and hopefully, I think always—at least frequently will return that money, will say they dis-
agree with the source of the money. Hopefully all of
us will do that. But whether or not we all live up to
that standard, you clearly do not adopt that as a standard for contributions to Mariam's Appeal. You're
not going to look at the source of the money;
you're just simply going to accept the money, and
you've made that clear.

I wanted just to ask you about Tariq Aziz.

GALLOWAY: Yeah.

SEN. LEVIN: Tariq Aziz. You've indicated you, you—who you didn't talk to and who you did talk to. Did you have conversations with Tariq Aziz about the award of oil allocations? That's my question.

GALLOWAY: Never.

SEN. LEVIN: Thank you. I'm done. Thank you.

SEN. COLEMAN: Just one follow-up on the Tariq Aziz question. How often did you uh . . . Can you describe the relation with Tariq Aziz?

GALLOWAY: Friendly.

SEN. COLEMAN: How often did you meet him?

GALLOWAY: Many times.

SEN. COLEMAN: Can you give an estimate of that?

GALLOWAY: No. Many times.

SEN. COLEMAN: Is it more than five?

GALLOWAY: Yes, sir.

SEN. COLEMAN: More than ten?

GALLOWAY: Yes.

SEN. COLEMAN: Fifteen? Around fifteen?

GALLOWAY: Well, we're getting nearer, but I haven't counted. But many times. I'm saying to you "Many times," and I'm saying to you that I was friendly with him.

SEN. COLEMAN: And you describe him as "a very dear friend"?

GALLOWAY: I think you've quoted me as saying "a dear, dear friend." I don't often use the double adjective, but—

SEN. COLEMAN: —I was looking into your heart on that.—

GALLOWAY:—but "friend" I have no problem with.

Senator, just before you go on—I do hope that you'll avail yourself of this dossier that I have produced. And I am really speaking through you to Senator Levin. This is what I have said about Saddam Hussein.

SEN. COLEMAN: Well, we'll enter that into the record without objection. I have no further questions of the witness. You're excused, Mr. Galloway.

GALLOWAY: Thank you very much.